LOTTERIES

Who Wins, Who Loses?

LOTTERIES
Who Wins, Who Loses?

Ann E. Weiss

—Issues in Focus—

ENSLOW PUBLISHERS, INC.

Bloy St. and Ramsey Ave.	P.O. Box 38
Box 777	Aldershot
Hillside, N.J. 07205	Hants GU12 6BP
U.S.A.	U.K.

For Malcolm

Library of Congress Cataloging-In-Publication Data

Weiss, Ann E., 1943-
  Lotteries: who wins, who loses?/Ann E. Weiss.

    p. cm. — (Issues in focus)

  Includes bibliographical references and index.

  ISBN 0-89490-242-3

    1. Lotteries—United States. I. Title. II. Series: Issues in
focus (Hillside, N.J.)

HG6126.W45 1991
336.1'0973—dc20   90-26525
                                                   CIP

Printed in the United States of America

10 9 8 7 6 5 4 3 2

Contents

1

"Zillions!"

When Curtis Sharpe won $5 million in the New York State lottery, the news made national headlines. From mailroom clerk at Bell Laboratories in New Jersey to multimillionaire overnight—Sharpe's transformation was everyone's dream come true. Flashbulbs popped and reporters shouted their eager questions as the debonair winner, with his soon-to-be ex-wife Barbara on one arm and fiancée Jackie on the other, showed up at lottery headquarters to have his ticket validated. Photos of Sharpe accepting his first $198,000 check—he would receive the balance of his prize money in nineteen annual equally large installments—appeared in newspapers and magazines and on television screens around the country. In the weeks that followed his win, Americans continued to read and hear about Sharpe's doings: his final divorce decree and marriage to Jackie—the bride wore a $13,000 dress, and the nuptial festivities carried a price tag to match—the couple's fourteen-room, $175,000 house, their new Cadillac complete with a $5,000 car-phone system, their collection of diamond jewelry. . . . Becoming a $5 million state lottery winner had made Curtis Sharpe big news indeed.

Deloise Singletary, on the other hand, wasn't particularly big news when she won even more, $5.5 million, in the Maryland State lottery. Granted, the fifty-eight-year-old mother of four was a less flamboyant character than Sharpe. Nevertheless, her change in lifestyle—from unskilled odd-jobs worker living in rented apartments and relying on public transportation to the leisured owner of a stylish suburban home with a Mercedes-Benz in the garage—was surely as remarkable as his. So why wasn't it as widely reported?

And why wasn't it particularly newsworthy when four people, each with the same winning combination of numbers, split a $21-million jackpot in Illinois? Four $5 million-plus winners in a single day—and not news? What was going on here?

The answer can be summed up in three dates: 1983, 1984, and 1988.

It was in 1983 that Curtis Sharpe experienced his incredible good fortune. At the time, it really did seem incredible. Since the 1960s, when New Hampshire became the first state in the twentieth century to authorize a legal lottery, even the top prizes had been reckoned in the mere hundreds of thousands of dollars. By the 1980s, though, the number of million- and multimillion-dollar wins was escalating. It was in January of 1984 that Deloise Singletary's win outstripped Sharpe's. Later that year, a Chicago printer won $40 million, and in 1985, a computer analyst from Brooklyn, New York, took home $13 million. Wins that had once seemed impossibly huge were beginning to sound like old news.

That was the reason for the four-way $21-million split in Illinois going almost unnoticed in the national news media. It came on September 3, 1988. That was also the date a twenty-nine-year-old New York truck driver won $23 million in his state's lottery—*and* when a real estate agent named Sheelah Ryan drew a prize of $55.16 million in Florida. In a single, stunning day, lucky players had walked off with nearly $100 million. "Zillions!" shrieked the headline in one newspaper, a New York City tabloid, the *Daily News*. Lottery fever—some called it "lottomania"—had gripped the nation.

Lottery Fever

Lottomania showed no sign of abating as the United States entered the 1990s. Among its symptoms are those ever-growing jackpots. The size of a lottery jackpot depends entirely upon the number of tickets sold. The more people who buy—and the more tickets each buyer purchases—the larger the pot becomes. The larger it becomes, the more people will buy additional tickets, and the bigger the pot grows. As it grows, so does the excitement, and that excitement stimulates further sales. On October 28, 1988, the California jackpot hit the $30.48 million mark. The next day, the day set for the drawing, eager buyers grabbed up another $31.5 million worth of tickets. A year later, with the state's jackpot at about $50 million, Californians were buying over a million chances an hour—during the slow hours of the day. When, at about the same time, the Pennsylvania prize soared to a record $115 million, men and women from all across the country flocked to the state for tickets. (By law, lottery tickets may not be sold across state lines.)

The long lines at lottery machines—and greater and greater cash outlays for tickets—are another symptom of lottomania. New Hampshire made its first ticket sale on March 12, 1964. By 1980, according to the U.S. Census Bureau, thirteen states were pulling in a yearly $2.2 billion. Ten years later, thirty-two states, the District of Columbia, Puerto Rico, and the U.S. Virgin Islands were combining for sales of over $17 billion. The fact that the number of states with lotteries keeps going up is, of course, yet another sign of lottery fever. Lotteries opened in four states as recently as 1990.

Why the passion for lotteries as the United States prepares to enter the twenty-first century? In the first place, they're fun. Most Americans think of lotteries as an inexpensive form of entertainment. A dollar isn't much to spend for a dream, they say, and what a dream! Imagine the thrill of becoming the next Sheelah Ryan—or even the next Curtis Sharpe. And it's an intriguing challenge for individual players to try to figure out the exact combination of numbers that will prove lucky for them.

As far as the sponsoring states are concerned, lotteries have a purpose beyond entertainment. They are serious fund-raisers. About half the money a state collects in ticket sales goes to help pay for state services. Some states spend their lottery revenues on public education or care for the elderly, while others apply it to the general fund. Money earned through a state lottery is money that does not have to be raised by increasing people's taxes, and state lawmakers have learned that, whereas voters will resist any tax hike, they will wait impatiently in line to buy lottery tickets.

If people are eager to substitute lotteries for taxes on the state level, some suggest, why not try it on the federal level? The U.S. Treasury is desperate for money; the national debt amounted to over $3 trillion in 1990. Some Americans say a national lottery could be just what's needed to start reducing that debt. In a 1989 article in *Fortune* magazine, Alvin Rabushka and Mikhail S. Bernstam, researchers at Washington, D.C.'s conservative Hoover Institution predicted receipts of more than $18 billion yearly from such a scheme.

A Dangerous Fever?

Not everyone is convinced that a national lottery is such a good idea. State lotteries have their critics, too.

Men and women who oppose lotteries have several points to make. The games are unfair to those who play them, they say, since, out of what is collected from ticket sales, most states return only 50 percent or less in prizes. It's also unfair to call lotteries "games," the critics go on, since they are really taxes in disguise. What is more, they are taxes that hit the poorest part of the population especially hard. A dollar lottery ticket takes a bigger percentage out of a $15,000-a-year budget than out of a $30,000-a-year one. Lotteries can be unfair even to those who win them, some think. Big winners may not be prepared to handle sudden wealth and all the pressures that go along with it. Five years after his win, for instance, Curtis Sharpe's wild spending had reportedly landed him in debt. It was certainly a fact that his Cadillac had been stolen and not replaced and that he and Jackie had separated. Another multimillion-dollar New York winner collected his first lottery payoff, quit his $38,000-a-year job, and put $10,000 down on each of ten luxury cars. Eight months later, six of the vehicles had been repossessed, and the man owed his creditors $200,000.

Lottery opponents further point out that lotteries are a form of gambling. Should governments be in the position of sponsoring gambling? they ask. Should governments be telling people, through lottery promotion and advertising, that the road to success has more to do with luck and chance than with hard work and sound moral values? It was upon such values that this country was founded and through hard work that it prospered. Can Americans preserve their values and thrive as a people—and continue to cultivate lottery fever?

2

Where "Profite Doth With Pleasure Joyne . . ."

A lottery, says the *Columbia Viking Desk Encyclopedia,* is a "scheme for distributing prizes by lot or other method of chance selection to persons who have paid for the opportunity to win." That definition perfectly describes modern state lottery systems. A person buys a ticket—or tickets—picks a number or numbers—or relies upon a computer to do the picking—and hopes that number or numbers will turn up lucky. If it does, the ticket holder may win anything from a free new ticket to millions of dollars.

Lotteries, including state-run lotteries, are perhaps the most widespread form of gambling in the United States today and go by various names—sweepstakes, raffles, and bingo, among them. They are characterized by the fact that they are games of pure chance, involving no element of skill. It is this that distinguishes them from those types of gambling in which knowledge or expertise can increase the likelihood of winning. Careful racetrack gamblers, for example, make their bets based upon such factors as the speed and strength of the animals, or by studying track and weather conditions. Successful poker players trust to their card-handling proficiency as much as to the chance of the draw. But lottery players have only blind luck on their side. Nothing they can do will make it more likely that their number will come up a winner—provided, of course, that the lottery is an honest one and has not been "fixed" ahead of time. Lottery winners and losers are determined by chance and chance alone.

In that, lotteries are rather like life itself. True, life involves more than mere randomness. A woman who graduates from college and goes on to study law is more likely to become a successful attorney than one who drops out of high school at age sixteen. A man whose hobby is skydiving may be more apt to suffer an injury than one who spends his free time in front of the TV set. Still, athlete and couch potato are equally likely, or unlikely, to be in the wrong spot at the wrong time when a car hurtles down the freeway at ninety miles an hour, bearing death and destruction. The dropout and the lawyer buy the same kind of canned soup in the same supermarket on the same day. One happens to pick up the can contaminated with the organism that causes botulism poisoning; the other happens not to. Or, as the Bible says, in the Old Testament book of Ecclesiastes, ". . . the race is not to the swift, nor the battle to the strong, neither yet bread to the wise, nor yet riches to men of understanding, nor yet favour to men of skill; but time and chance happeneth to them all."

The Appeal of Lotteries

It is God, the Old Testament makes clear, who possesses the ultimate power to decide how that chance will fall out. It is he who decides which person will die on the freeway and whose hand reaches toward the deadly can. God decides much else besides, right down to the tiniest, most insignificant-seeming details of daily life. And, having the power to order those details, God sometimes arranges them to reveal his will to human beings here on earth. The story of Jonah and the whale illustrates how this can happen.

According to the book of Jonah, God commanded Jonah to go to the wicked city of Nineveh to preach repentance to its people. The reluctant Jonah sought to avoid the mission by fleeing to sea in a ship.

Then God sent a great storm "so that the ship was like to be broken." The frightened sailors, aware that the tempest was a sign of God's anger against someone on board but not knowing who that person might be, threw lots to find out. The lot fell to Jonah. Or rather, God *caused* the lot to fall to Jonah. The sailors, and Jonah himself, recognized the meaning of that. "Cast me forth into the sea," Jonah urged his shipmates, "so shall the sea be calm unto you: for I know that for my sake this great tempest is upon you." Jonah was tossed overboard, to be swallowed by a great fish, and the sea ceased its raging. Later, after having been delivered from the fish, Jonah did preach in Nineveh. The city repented of its sins, and God spared it.

The long-ago Hebrews were not alone in the their belief that the drawing of lots has a religious dimension, and peoples in many different times and places have used the practice to find the answers to important questions or to learn how God, or the gods, wanted them to act in certain situations. The Anglo-Saxons, Germanic tribesmen who began settling in England in the fifth century A.D. were one such people. In fact, it was they who gave us the word "lot," from their *hlot,* a counter or marker used to determine a matter by chance.

The people of the ancient city-state of Rome were similarly familiar with lotteries. Hundreds of years before the Anglo-Saxons began their westward expansion, Roman rulers employed a kind of lottery to help keep peace in their empire, which stretched across Europe from the Near East to northern England. If a town or a tribe rebelled against Roman authority, its men were rounded up and herded into some public place. There, imperial soldiers lined the captives up in random order and arbitrarily executed every tenth one. It is from this form of punishment-by-lot that our word "decimate," from the Latin *decim*, meaning ten, derives.

In the modern world, too, people have turned to lotteries to decide matters of life and death. During World War II (1941–1945) and again when the United States was involved in fighting in the Southeast Asian nation of Vietnam (1964–1973), U.S. Army officials used a lottery to determine which draft-eligible young Americans would be required to serve in the military—and which would escape duty. Only with the end of the war in Vietnam did the country abandon the draft lottery in favor of an all-volunteer army, such as the one used in the 1991 Persian Gulf War.

Even now, people use lotteries to make other types of decisions, some momentous, some trivial. Neighborhood youngsters may draw straws to choose sides for stickball. Friends toss a coin or a pair of dice to settle who goes first in a game. Soldiers may use similar methods to decide which one leads the way into a suspected minefield. Picking the person to be "it" in a game of tag by chanting, "Eeeny, meeny, miney, mo . . . Out goes Y-O-U," distantly echoes the Roman habit of decimating a town in rebellion. When new apartments open up in a big-city public housing project, applicants for those living spaces may be weeded out by means of a lottery. In the same way, contestants in New York City's yearly marathon are selected in a multipart lottery process. That's the most evenhanded way, race officials believe, of narrowing the field of runners to a manageable number. We today may be living on the brink of the twenty-first century, but we have not lost that primitive sense that "time and chance happeneth to all men" and that a lottery is somehow supremely fair, its very random impartiality reflective of the randomness of all life. Somewhere deep within us, there lingers the feeling that God—or providence, or fate—controls the draw and that its outcome is therefore a revelation of divine will. With this thought in mind, try reading "The Lottery," a classic short story by American author Shirley Jackson.

Lotteries in the Old World

Of course, lotteries appeal to human beings on more than religious grounds. As we saw in Chapter 1, they are also a form of entertainment and have been since at least as long ago as the days of the Roman Empire. When the emperor Nero, who ruled from A.D. 54 to A.D. 68, gave dinner parties, he sometimes invited his guests to draw for such prizes as slaves or a villa in the country. A century and a half later, another emperor, Heliogabalus, livened up the contests—or tried to—by including as "prizes" items like dead animals and insects. Still later, during Europe's Middle Ages, which lasted from about the year 800 to around 1400, lotteries were a common feature at fairs and festivals.

Besides being entertaining, a lottery may be profitable, not only to its winner, but also to the individual or group that runs it. That is because, typically, only a part of the money paid into the jackpot is returned in prizes. As we saw in Chapter 1, much of the unreturned portion in today's U.S. state-sponsored lotteries goes to help support such public enterprises as education or health care. In older times, too, lottery profits might be directed toward public improvements or private ventures. The first Roman emperor, Caesar Augustus (ruled 29 B.C. to A.D. 14), instituted a lottery whose after-prize proceeds he spent on repairing the city, which had been damaged during two decades of civil war. Throughout the Middle Ages, Europe's hundreds of local feudal lords and princes sponsored informal lotteries, using them as fund-raisers for castle upkeep, improved fortifications, and the like. Church officials, always in need of money to build and run hospitals, orphanages, and other charitable institutions, or to add to building and maintenance funds, held drawings from time to time. Modern church bingo nights are a reminder of those medieval games.

By the year 1500, the Middle Ages had ended and the modern world was taking shape. City-states were merging into nations, squabbling local lords submitting to strong monarchs, and feudal principalities being replaced by centralized governments. Economies were no longer primarily dependent upon farming; business was expanding and the barter of goods giving way to the use of money. Serfs and peasants were winning their freedom and trading the quiet countryside for city life. Through all the changes, lotteries remained as popular as ever. Now, though, they were being run along more businesslike lines, and governments were finding ways to benefit from them.

It was in Italy that lotteries were first run on a more regular basis and in a professional way. The trend toward professionalism quickly reached Germany, Austria, and France, and in 1539, France became the first place where the state sought to profit from the games. From there, state involvement spread to England. The first official English lottery was authorized in 1566 by Queen Elizabeth I as a means of financing improvements to the nation's harbors. Later, public lotteries helped to supply London with water, build a bridge across the city's Thames River, and finance the establishment of the British Museum.

In private lotteries also, state involvement became the rule. Sponsors were required to obtain government licenses, and their proceeds were subject to a tax. As in the past, private lotteries raised money for local or charitable causes, but increasingly, they were also employed by merchants eager to dispose of their goods. Even though money was more readily available in the 1500s than it had been earlier, expensive merchandise often remained unsold since only the very wealthiest could afford its cost. But lottery tickets came cheap, and even commoners could usually lay their hands on a coin or two with which to purchase the chance of winning a prize that would otherwise have been beyond their means. Lotteries thus allowed businessmen to "sell" at a good price even in a cash-poor society.

New World Lotteries

In the next century, lotteries took on a new function, that of speeding the colonization of North America. The first English attempt to plant a New World colony came with the settlement of Roanoke Island, off what is now North Carolina, in 1585. That colony failed, and its few members vanished without a trace. Twenty-two years later, an effort to colonize the cold and stormy coast of Maine also failed. But by the time it did, 105 Englishmen had already landed at Jamestown, Virginia.

At first, Jamestown, too, seemed doomed. Seventy-three settlers died during the first winter, and the town came under attack by Native Americans. The Spanish attacked as well—Spain was England's archenemy in those days—and the threat of starvation was never distant. Although the settlement was resupplied yearly by the Virginia Company, the private English corporation that owned it, company officials were unwilling, or unable, to provide help on the scale needed. Then, in 1612, those officials decided to apply to the crown for a license to run a raffle, the proceeds of which would go to Jamestown. The license was granted.

In all, four Jamestown raffles were held. The first was won by a London tailor, whose prize of "foure thousands crownes [worth of] fayre plate [silver table settings] was sent to his house in very stately manner." Word of the win helped advertise the lottery and encouraged others to buy into it. Publication of a ballad probably helped, too:

> *"Heere profite doth with pleasure joyne,*
> *and bids each chearefull heart,*
> *To this high praysed enterprise,*
> *performe a Christian part . . . "*

Not only were ticket buyers serving religion by ensuring Christian settlement in America, they were assured, but they were also serving

19

their country, and, thereby, themselves. There could be no losers in this lottery:

> *"Let no man thinke that he shall loose,*
> *though he no Prize poscesse:*
> *His substaunce to Virginia goes,*
> *which God, no doubt will blesse."*

The combined appeal to religion and patriotism boosted lottery sales, and fortune did begin smiling upon Jamestown. By 1613, the colony was stabilizing. In 1614, the Virginia Company rewrote its rules, making it possible for the settlers to buy and own land. The colonists learned to cultivate tobacco and began sending regular shipments back to England. In 1617, more women joined the settlers, and the year after that, the colony gained a measure of self-rule. Jamestown had become self-sustaining, and profits were flowing into the pockets of Virginia Company stockholders. Captain John Smith, one of the settlement's early leaders, did not hesitate to credit the lottery for the colony's new profitability. The raffles had, he said, been "the real and substantiall food, by which Virginia hath been nourished."

Yet there were criticisms to be heard. Some charged that the Virginia Company had mismanaged the lottery and allowed fraud to affect the results of its drawings. Others worried about the games' effect on "the Common sort" of English men and women. Were the poor squandering their pennies on tickets, getting into the habit of trusting to luck—rather than to hard work—to get ahead? Another concern was that the raffle might be making England look foolish in the eyes of the world. Already the Spanish were sniggering, saying that English New World colonization was a pretty feeble affair if it depended upon "a generall kynde of begging."

The final criticism, and perhaps the most telling one, was that the lottery was supporting a private purpose, not a public one. Ticket sales were being solicited in the name of God and country, but the end result was filling Virginia Company coffers. Was it right, English lawmakers in Parliament asked, for ordinary Londoners to be "drayned" for the benefit of a few rich men? They thought not, and on March 8, 1621, King James I withdrew the Virginia Company's lottery license. It soon became apparent that company officials had relied overmuch on the raffle as a source of income. In 1624, they were forced into bankruptcy, and the company was dissolved.

The end of the Jamestown lottery did nothing to stop gambling in the New World. In the southern colonies, particularly, games of chance were popular and growing more so, as was betting on cards or horse races. Settlers in that part of North America retained the English way of thinking about gambling—that it was acceptable as long as it involved neither cheating nor disturbing the peace. They further shared the English notion that gambling is more appropriate in members of the upper classes than among those of lower social and economic rank. In Virginia, as in the mother country, the sport was a "gentleman's privilege," except for a few days during the Christmas season, when the common folk might join in.

In such northern colonies as Pennsylvania and Massachusetts, attitudes toward gambling were less relaxed. In Pennsylvania, colonized in the 1680s by members of the Society of Friends, or Quakers, gaming was viewed as an inducement to godlessness and idleness. Between 1682 and 1740, the God-fearing, industrious Quakers attempted to enforce laws aimed at discouraging all forms of the vice.

Among the Pilgrims and Puritans of Massachusetts, antigambling sentiment was, if anything, even more pronounced. Puritans took seriously the idea that God involved himself in every earthly event, no matter how unimportant it might appear to be. That involvement meant that any gamble—from the casting of lots by Jonah's shipmates to a bet on a race or the purchase of lottery ticket—constituted an appeal to God's judgment. In the case of Jonah, the making of that appeal was justified by the seriousness of the situation, but gambling for fun did not merit the attention of Divine Providence. Worse, it mocked Providence by trivializing it. Early Puritan prohibitions against gambling, including the establishment of lotteries, were strict.

They did not remain so for long, and in Pennsylvania, too, the effort to eliminate gambling proved futile. The original Quaker settlers were soon outnumbered in Pennsylvania, and so were the Puritans in Massachusetts, and as the population of each colony grew more varied, public ideas changed. By 1715 or so, the authorities were finding it difficult to make their antigambling statutes stick, and by mid-century, lotteries in every colony were helping to support education, maintain charities, and subsidize municipal improvements. In 1744, for example, Rhode Island authorized a lottery to pay for building a bridge over the Woboset River in Providence. New York City held a lottery two years later to raise money to fortify the town. Another 1746 New York lottery provided funds for the establishment of King's College, now known as Columbia University. Still other lotteries helped to found and support Harvard College, Yale, Dartmouth, and Williams. After Boston's Faneuil Hall marketplace burned in 1741, it was rebuilt courtesy of a raffle. Twelve years later, parishioners at Philadelphia's Christ Church bought a new steeple with lottery proceeds. By then, Philadelphia's financial position was so precarious that the city itself was investing in lottery tickets.

Why were lotteries so popular in the American colonies of the eighteenth century? For the same reasons they had been popular in years gone by—and remain so today. First, people found them fun to play. Second, the colonial lotteries were local affairs that benefited local causes, making even losers feel like winners. In 1772, proceeds from a single drawing on Pettie's Island in the Delaware River reportedly went in equal portions to nearby Presbyterian and Lutheran churches, to the Newark (New Jersey) Academy, and to "three Schoolmasters in Philadelphia." How many area churchgoers benefited from that lottery—even if they didn't happen to hold a winning ticket? How many of their children were helped to an education? The third reason for the games' popularity, in colonial times as now, was that they offered what many thought of as an attractive alternative to new taxes.

Even in wartime, lotteries were allowed to substitute for tax increases. During the French and Indian Wars of the 1750s and 1760s, in which England and her colonies fought against the French and their Native American allies, lotteries were held to raise money for the support of the English-American army. In 1777, after the colonists declared their independence from England and the American Revolution had begun, Congress voted in favor of a lottery to help fund that war effort. This congressional expedient won the approval of individuals of such varied backgrounds as gentleman farmer and military man George Washington; businessman John Hancock; and printer, scientist, and philosopher Benjamin Franklin.

Supporters of the 1777 lottery, which was to consist of four separate drawings, urged participation on patriotic grounds. "It is not doubted," read one advertisement, "but every real friend of his country will most cheerfully become an adventurer, and that the sale of tickets will be very rapid, especially as even the unsuccessful adventurer will have the pleasing reflection of having contributed a degree to the great and glorious American cause." Alas for that ad-writer's hopes. Tickets sold poorly, and the lottery produced little profit.

Lotteries in the New Nation

The Revolution over and independence won, the new United States continued to rely upon lotteries to pay for public amenities and services that its people might otherwise have had to do without. This reliance was necessitated by the citizenry's determination to avoid taxation. As historian John Bach McMaster described the mood of the day, "taxes, the people would not bear." To add to their economic woes, the states and cities of 200 years ago were hardly in a position to raise badly needed funds by borrowing. So financially strapped were they that few banks or wealthy individuals would risk lending to them. So what other alternatives were there but lotteries? Finally, and as always, lotteries, like other forms of gambling, were fun.

Fun in a fashion and to a degree perhaps unique to the young country. As we have seen, there is something about a lottery that appeals deeply to the human spirit. And there is, it seems, something in the American soul especially that responds to the opportunity to take a chance, to risk all on a dare. Maybe that is because America is in a sense a nation founded upon a series of gambles.

It was a gamble for those English men and women who settled, nearly four centuries ago, on Roanoke Island and on the coast of Maine and at Jamestown. It was a gamble many lost, though some, like George Washington's ancestor John, who landed in Virginia in 1657, came up winners. It was a gamble for the French and Spanish explorers who sailed to the New World in search of fame and fortune. Some found it. Others perished in the wilderness. It was a gamble for English Catholics sponsored by George Calvert, Lord Baltimore, to set out for America in search of religious freedom in 1632. It was a gamble, in the 1700s, to seek new frontiers, in western Pennsylvania, in the Blue Ridge Mountains of North Carolina, in Kentucky and Ohio—a gamble that paid off for thousands in rich farmland, valuable pelts of fur, and rolling hills and valleys in which to raise horses and cattle. In the next century, it became a gamble to stake a claim in the West, to avail oneself of government land giveaways, to search out veins of mineral ores, to start a business or set up a factory in a booming East Coast city, or to sink all one's cash into a risky venture like the building of a railroad.

Many have made the comparison between the settling of America and the placing of a wager. Laura Ingalls Wilder, in her "Little House" stories, tells how Pa refers to winning his "bet" with Uncle Sam and earning permanent title to his 160 acres on the South Dakota prairie. Of course, Pa's bet was more complex than the kind of bet involved in buying a lottery ticket. Proving up on the homestead demanded more than luck; it meant working hard and braving great dangers. But it took luck, as well. To win security for himself and his family, Pa had to test his fortune against blizzards, tornadoes, and drought, against failed crops, food shortages, and thieves in the night. The moment the Ingallses left the relative safety of their home in the Big Woods of Wisconsin, they stepped into a sort of real-life game of chance.

University of Pennsylvania history professor John M. Findlay has similarly compared pioneering to wagering. In his book, *People of Chance,* Findlay details the connection: "Like bettors, pioneers have repeatedly grasped the chance to get something for nothing—to claim free land, to pick up nuggets of gold, to speculate on western real estate . . . Frontiersmen have cherished risks in order to get ahead . . . migrants to new territories have sought to begin again in a setting that made all participants equal at the start . . ."

Yet that pioneering willingness to take a chance or place a bet has always been counterbalanced by the uneasy sense that there is something wrong and sinful about gambling. Americans have never quite forgotten that old Quaker equation that links the sport with idleness, nor shaken the Puritan conviction that it amounts to an unforgivable trifling with the Divine. The conflict between the two points of view—present since colonial days—intensified in the first half of the nineteenth century.

On the one hand, lotteries flourished well into the century. Eager bettors flocked to buy tickets, and by 1832, New York City had 160 shops in which chances might be purchased. Philadelphia had 200. States and cities were still doing a brisk business in lottery licenses. Between 1790 and 1860, permits were issued to 50 colleges, 300 lower schools, and 200 churches. Other lotteries were licensed to support the construction of bridges, roads, and canals.

As time passed, the lotteries were more and more likely to be organized and run, not by local people or institutions, but by lottery professionals. These professionals were contractors who operated on a statewide basis, or on an even larger, regional one. Unlike the lotteries of colonial times, these games were big business. Participants were no longer buying tickets from friends and neighbors and people they knew, but from strangers. Increasingly, those strangers were brokers, who purchased great numbers of tickets at a discount for resale to the public. In many instances, the brokers worked directly for the lottery contractors. The trend toward centralization proceeded rapidly, and by the 1830s, five or six companies had come to dominate lottery action around the country. The early 1800s were indeed boom years for the lottery industry.

The Boom Years—and a Push for Reform

Yet those same years saw the games attacked by a growing regiment of critics. Some objected to the games on religious grounds. Interestingly, the religion was neither Puritan nor Quaker, and it was centered, not in the North, but in the South. That part of the country, once so hospitable to gamblers, had changed. In the years leading up to the American Revolution, many members of the Baptist faith had migrated to the area. Southern Baptists were characterized, in the words of one observer, by their commitment to "ardent Pray'r . . . & an active Banishment of Gaming, Dancing, & Sabbath-Day Diversions." Over time, the Baptist influence transformed the Southern "Bible Belt" from part of the nation that most widely supported gambling to that part most adamantly opposed to it on religious principle.

Another objection to lotteries, this one less specifically religious and more broadly ethical, came from the ranks of the many reform-minded men and women of the first half of the nineteenth century. The reformers interested themselves in a number of causes: Abolition (putting an end to the human slavery that still existed in the South); Temperance (halting the sale and consumption of alcoholic beverages); Female rights (allowing women to seek a greater and more equal role in society). Generally speaking, each of these reform goals was founded on an ideal of personal freedom: the slave's freedom to enjoy the fruits of his labor; a family's freedom from the curse of drunkenness; a woman's freedom to control her own life and future.

As the reformers saw it, eliminating public and private lotteries would similarly enhance the personal freedom of Americans. How? In the first place, by liberating them from what many regarded as a form of slavery. "No affrican," a Virginia Planter named Landon Carter had written a few decades earlier, "is so great a Slave" as someone with a "Passion for gambling." Not everyone will agree with that assessment, but the reformers, perhaps thinking of the kind of people we today would call compulsive or addicted gamblers, did.

An end to lotteries would, the reformers thought, also lead to improvements in the economic standing of thousands of the poor and working class. How many struggling office clerks, outdoor laborers, and overworked factory girls were wasting their paltry wages on lottery tickets? they asked. Their answer: plenty. And why were the lower classes throwing away their hard-earned dollars on the remote chance of winning? Partly because government encouraged them to. Needing tax money but unwilling to rouse public wrath by imposing revenue measures in an open and aboveboard fashion, the nation's leaders were wringing tax substitutes out of the pockets of those who could least afford to pay them. "Who pays the oppressive Tax . . . ?" lottery critic Thomas Man thundered in 1833. "The industrious Mechanic—the hardy Tiller of the Soil. It is the small pittance wrung from the common laborer who lives by the sweat of his brow . . . it is bread taken from the mouths of his children . . . " Man ended with a plea to Americans to do away with the "Horrid Monster" that lotteries had become. "Crush the *Damned Monster*, or away—your vaunted *Liberty* and *Freedom*."

But government was not alone in promoting lottery activity and depriving children of sustenance, the reformers told the country. Monopolistic lottery contractors and brokers were doing their part as well. To attract those who couldn't afford the price of a whole chance, for example, brokers would divide the ticket into shares. People could buy as much as half a share or as little as one-eighth. Or they could "rent" a ticket for a day, hoping against hope that the twenty-four-hour period they chose would be the one during which that ticket's number would come up. A day's ticket rental cost 50 cents.

For those unable to afford even that amount of money, there were other gambling possibilities. Unlicensed "numbers" games, also known as "insurance" or "policy" games, were making their way into big-city neighborhoods. These games gave people a chance to bet what number would come in the legal lottery, and they let them do so for mere pennies. Numbers rackets, although strictly against the law, remain common around the country. And they developed, lottery critics pointed out—and still point out today—directly out of legal schemes.

Not only were legal lotteries giving rise to unlicensed, and hence illegal, games, but even licensed lotteries were succumbing to fraud and corruption. Winning lottery numbers were supposed to be determined by the drawing of numbered balls from a large wheel-shaped hopper. In some instances, those charged with selecting the balls committed fraud by deciding ahead of time what the "lucky" number would be, hiding balls bearing those numbers up their sleeves, and allowing the balls to slide into their hands at the appropriate moment. In other cases, ticket sellers sold number combinations that had already—and unbeknownst to the unfortunate buyers—been drawn. Nor was the forging of "winning" tickets uncommon.

Yet another concern of lottery critics was that less and less of the proceeds was going to the public purpose for which it was supposed to be intended. In 1819, New York's General Assembly learned to its dismay that the state had lost over $100,000 on its licensed lotteries. "The only recommendation of the system of raising money by lottery," said one disgruntled lawmaker, "is the cheerfulness with which it is paid." In Pennsylvania, a lottery organized to provide construction funds for the Union Canal Company took in a total of $21,246,891 over an eighteen-year period. Of that amount, only $405,460—less than 2 percent of the total—went to canal building. Some went to prizewinners, but the bulk of the take ended up with the professionals running the lottery.

An End to Lotteries

By the end of the century's second decade, the states were beginning to act against lottery abuses. In 1819, New York legislators banned unlicensed numbers games, set a ten-year prison term for anyone found guilty of forging tickets, and, in an effort to ensure honest drawings, required those who selected the numbered balls to leave their arms bare. The laws did little to end the corruption, however, and in 1830, a state grand jury charged with investigating lotteries called them a "vile tax on the needy and ignorant" and called for outlawing them altogether. This New York did, effective December 31, 1833. It was the third state to do so, Massachusetts and Pennsylvania having acted earlier that same year. Ohio, Vermont, Maine, New Jersey, New Hampshire, and Illinois followed suit the next year. Nor did the states simply enact antilottery laws. Most went so far as to amend their state constitutions to forbid them, and by the end of the century, thirty-six of the forty-five states then in the Union had enacted constitutional lottery bans. England, too, outlawed the games, except for those held principally to benefit a charity. The English ban came in 1823.

By the time the American Civil War began in 1861, lotteries were illegal around the United States. The war, a bloody struggle between North and South that resulted in the preservation of the Union and the abolition of slavery, ended in 1865. With its conclusion came the country's final nineteenth century venture into legal lottery activity. On January 1, 1869, the state of Louisiana issued a lottery charter to a company in that state.

The Louisiana Lottery Company was notorious from the outset. Although company officials claimed to be going into business to benefit a New Orleans charity hospital, few accepted that claim as true. Opposition to the enterprise was so strong that the Louisiana company had to pay $50,000 in bribes to get state legislators to approve its charter. Over the next seven years, another $300,000 went out in illegal payoffs. In addition, in order to maintain its facade of being a legitimate charitable operation, the lottery found itself donating $40,000 a year to the hospital.

Given such tremendous overhead costs, the Louisiana Lottery had to attract as many ticket buyers as it possibly could. Lottery ads appeared in newspapers around the country, and envelopes containing cash began pouring in at the rate of 8,000 a day. Besides its chartered activities, the company ran a low-cost unlicensed numbers game on the side. As its profits rose, the lottery's parent company invested in banks, land, sugar refineries, and other businesses, eventually attaining an income of about $30,000,000 a year. A generous portion of this amount continued to be used for bribes, not only to state lawmakers, but also to U.S. senators and judges. As a result of the illegal payoffs, Louisiana Lottery Company officials were able to dominate Louisiana politics for twenty years.

In April 1890, however, lottery officials finally went too far. They offered to pay the state $1,250,000 a year in return for charter renewal. One and a quarter million dollars was a tremendous sum a century ago. People around the country were outraged by the blatant corruption, and in Washington, D.C., U.S. President Benjamin Harrison appeared before Congress to attack the lottery. Even though the venture was state-chartered, he pointed out, its use of the U.S. mails made it a federal problem. "The people of all the states are debauched and defrauded . . . by the Louisiana Lottery," he declared. Harrison asked Congress for "severe and effectual legislation . . . to enable the Post Office Department to purge the mail of all letters, newspapers, and circulars relating to the business." Congress acted promptly, and the measure passed on September 19. Two years after that, the state of Louisiana itself banned lotteries.

For the next three-quarters of a century, there was no state-sponsored lottery activity in the United States.

3

"A Tax Laid on the Willing Only"

No one really expected it to happen, but it did. In 1963, New Hampshire state legislators passed a bill authorizing a twice-a-year sweepstakes contest. Tickets went on sale the next spring. After an almost eight-decade break, American government was back in the lottery business.

Not that the possibility of new government lotteries had been completely ignored over the years. During the 1930s, several lottery bills came before Congress and the legislatures of various states. The proposals grew largely out of the fact that the thirties were a time of financial disaster in the United States—and just about everywhere else. The stock market, the exchange where stocks, or shares, in business corporations are bought and sold, had crashed in October of 1929, and the price of shares plummeted. The world economy plummeted, too, into a deep depression. Businesses failed, factories closed down, and millions of people were left unemployed. Banks collapsed, and millions more found their life savings gone. Hundreds of thousands lost their homes and turned into wanderers, searching the country for a job, a bed, a meal. The country was broke.

What better time, many Americans asked, to reinstate official lotteries? They would bring in badly needed revenues—which were naturally down, since the jobless and homeless cannot pay much by way of taxes—and the proceeds might be used to provide some relief for the neediest. Not only that, but the games would offer the public a little low-cost fun, a ray of hope in a gray and desperate world. Despite such arguments, none of the bills became law. Memories of the scandal-ridden lotteries of the nineteenth century were still too vivid.

Nevertheless, suggestions for lotteries continued to be heard. In 1937, New Hampshire turned down one such proposal, and the next year, Maryland did the same. After December 1941, when the United States became involved in World War II, a new spate of lottery measures appeared before Congress and the state legislatures. Perhaps calling to mind the failed wartime ventures of 1777, lawmakers rejected all of them, and in 1944, the U.S. Department of the Treasury issued a strong antilottery statement. That put a temporary end to lottery talk at the federal level.

Yet even after 1945, when the war ended in victory for America and its allies and the nation entered a period of material prosperity, there were still those eager to see lotteries legalized. Lottery bills surfaced regularly in New Hampshire, and by the 1950s, calls for a national lottery, to be organized and run by the government in Washington, D.C., were appearing in a number of newspapers and magazines. Games of chance shouldn't be banned forever just because of a few unfortunate occurrences fifty or sixty years in the past, lottery advocates said. Besides, they added, other countries, like the Western European nations that had also outlawed the games because of nineteenth century concerns about morality, fraud, and the welfare of the poor, were now relaxing their restrictions. Wasn't it time for the United States to do the same?

It was true enough that state-sponsored lotteries had returned to Western Europe. A French lottery instituted in the depression year of 1933 provided benefits to veterans of World War I, for example. In 1934, the English Parliament made it easier for lottery sponsors to conduct games in the name of charity, and in the 1950s and 1960s, newer laws made claiming a charitable purpose easier still. English sports fans could also place legal bets on soccer contests. Soccer betting had become popular in Germany, the Scandinavian countries, and other nations, as well.

Another English scheme, one that enabled a lottery to double as a savings plan, was introduced in 1956. Under the British Premium Bond program, people buy special lottery bonds at banks and post offices. These bonds, like any others, earn interest, but instead of that interest being returned to each bondholder, it accumulates in a pool. Monthly drawings determine who wins the pool. Only a few winners are picked, of course, but losers retain their bonds, which they can either cash in at their original value or hang onto in hopes of being luckier next time.

England and the rest of Western Europe were not the only places with lotteries. A game was begun in Australia late in the 1800s but was at first a target of shutdown attempts. Not until several years into the twentieth century did contests there become firmly established. In some Australian states, a portion of lottery proceeds goes to charity. New Zealand, like Australia part of the British Commonwealth of Nations, had a state-sponsored charitable lottery, as well. Lotteries were also common throughout Latin America. The Mexican game, which dates back to 1771, is among the oldest anywhere. Top prize in that contest is known, appropriately enough, as "El Gordo," the fat one. Although Canada did not have a lottery until the province of Québec inaugurated one in 1970, it now boasts three all-Canada contests as well as provincial games. (Canadian provinces correspond to U.S. states.)

Even in the communist nations of Eastern Europe, people could buy chances in official pools and lotteries. After the Soviet Union came to dominate the area at the end of World War II, gambling of any kind was outlawed. By the late 1950s, though, the governments of countries like Poland and Hungary were sufficiently desperate for money to authorize fund-raising games. The Soviet Union itself instituted a lottery similar to England's Premium Bond program in order to pay for economic development in the wake of World War II. In fact, as U.S. lottery supporters were emphasizing at the start of the 1960s, state-run gambling in one form or another had become a fact of life practically worldwide. The United States and Canada, almost alone among nations, remained holdouts. Then came the New Hampshire legislature's surprising vote in favor of a state lottery, the proceeds of which were to go to public education.

The New Hampshire Lottery

The vote really did surprise observers. New Hampshire is in New England, and most Americans thought of New Englanders as steeped in the antigambling heritage of the area's original Puritan settlers. New Hampshire, in particular, struck outsiders as an unlikely place for a lottery to get started. They saw the state as rural and old-fashioned, inhabited by conservative Yankees prone to cling stubbornly to ideas about the value of thrift and hard work while scorning anything resembling a get-rich-quick scheme. New Hampshire's very nickname—the Granite State—seemed to speak of rock-ribbed attitudes and a stern way of life.

Even the New Hampshire legislators who approved the sweepstakes bill appeared somewhat startled by the turn of events. When they began their 1963 session, a solid majority of them had opposed the measure. But as the weeks slipped by, phone calls and letters poured into their offices from around the state. The bulk of the communications expressed strong support for a lottery. Bowing to constituent demand, legislator after legislator switched position on the issue. By the session's end, New Hampshire had its lottery.

And people around the country had a new—more accurate—picture of what New Hampshire was like. Contrary to popular opinion, the New Hampshire of the early 1960s was neither puritanical nor particularly rural. It certainly was not Yankee. Close to a third of its population was either foreign-born or first-generation American. Out of that third, the largest percentage had its roots in the French Canadian province of Québec. Remember that Québec would soon become the first part of Canada to establish a lottery. Furthermore, New Hampshire was 60 percent urban, and urban areas have generally proved more open to gambling than rural ones. As far as religion was concerned, nearly 40 percent of New Hampshire people were Roman Catholic. Of the country's major religious groups, Catholics have always been the most tolerant of gambling, and as we know, Catholic Church dependence upon lotteries to provide funds for charity and other purposes goes back hundreds of years. Add up New Hampshire's demographics, the statistics about its people—their religion, national origins, and degree of urbanization—and the result is obvious. Far from being among the least likely of states to take the lead in establishing the modern state lottery system, New Hampshire was among the most likely.

But demographics alone only partially explains why New Hampshire voters favored a lottery in 1963. To understand the other reasons, it is necessary to look at the state's unusual tax structure and at the way it has traditionally funded its public school system.

Unlike most other states, New Hampshire has neither a sales tax nor an income tax, and those are taxes New Hampshire people have resolved never to have. Of course, the state has other types of taxes. An inheritance tax requires anyone who receives a legacy to pay the state a percentage of its value. New Hampshire also has local property tax laws that apply to homeowners and to those holding other forms of real estate. Income from investments and interest on bank accounts may also be taxed.

Above all, though, New Hampshire has depended for revenue on so-called "sin taxes"—levies placed on the sale of such nonessential items as tobacco products, beer and wine, and hard liquor. The state also taxes the profits of its thriving horse-racing industry. Overall, in 1963, New Hampshire was getting a hefty 60 percent of its income from sin taxes.

A sweepstakes, its backers pointed out, would fit perfectly into this tax picture, since a state's lottery proceeds themselves amount to a sort of sin tax. No one forces anyone to gamble, after all, any more than anyone forces anyone else to drink or smoke. People who purchase state lottery tickets—thereby contributing to state revenues—do so of their own free choice. A lottery truly is what Thomas Jefferson, Founding Father and third U.S. president, called it: "A tax laid on the willing only"—exactly the kind best calculated to appeal to New Hampshire people.

Another advantage to a New Hampshire lottery, its proponents went on, was that it would give the state an opportunity to improve the quality of its public education. In 1963, New Hampshire schools lagged behind those of much of the rest of the nation, mostly, state educators maintained, because they were so poorly funded. Because there is no sales or income tax, those schools were supported almost entirely through local property taxes. So small, in fact, was the state's contribution to public education that New Hampshire ranked last in the nation—fiftieth out of fifty states—in terms of the proportion of state revenues turned over to help pay for local needs. A lottery, sweepstakes advocates said, would change that statistic. Under the terms of the bill before the legislature, all of the state's share of the proceeds would go to education. Pass the bill, and New Hampshire children would have good schools *without* their parents and neighbors having to pay the dread sales or income tax.

The arguments swayed the New Hampshire legislature—but would they convince the state's governor, John King, to sign the sweepstakes measure into law? Already, antilottery forces were at work trying to get him to reject it, for even in New Hampshire, public support for a lottery was not universal. The leaders of some Protestant churches spoke out against the idea on moral grounds. Law-enforcement officers and others worried that criminal elements, perhaps an organized crime syndicate, might try to seize control of any game. Even educators had their doubts about the scheme. Although they would be glad to see more money going to the state's school districts, they felt uneasy about the proposed source of that money. Lottery proceeds might fluctuate wildly, they warned, high one year, low the next. Instead of forcing the schools to live with such uncertainty, the state should redesign its tax structure so as to provide stable long-term funding for education. Finally, there were those with concerns about possible federal intervention if New Hampshire went ahead with a lottery. Congress had helped force the Louisiana Lottery Company out of business in 1890. Might it take similar action against a New Hampshire sweepstakes?

To the delight of lottery advocates, Governor King had little trouble dismissing such objections. Federal law could affect only lottery activity that crossed state lines or involved the use of the U.S. mails, he pointed out, and New Hampshire had no intention of running an interstate or mail-order game. The governor expressed every confidence that the lottery would stay honest and scoffed at the idea that organized crime might try to move in on it. Nor did he see much merit in moral objections to a sweepstakes.

King did, however, see a great deal of merit in a tax laid on the willing only. Although well aware that the schools were desperate for funds, he had no intention of following educators' suggestions regarding a restructuring of state taxes. "Restructuring," he felt sure, translated into "sales tax" or "income tax," and no New Hampshire governor could support either one and expect to survive in office. So Governor King did the politically wise thing. Proclaiming that New Hampshire was "already carrying a cross of taxation unequaled in American history," he announced his determination "to initiate programs which will relieve this heavy burden" on the people. New Hampshire got its sweepstakes.

It was no overnight success. As *Forbes* magazine writer James Cook put it, "The public yawned." Why? Because the game was boring. Drawings took place only once every six months, meaning, Cook wrote, "You bought a ticket, waited weeks or months for the winning number to be drawn, and probably ran out of patience." Excitement was close to nil, and ticket sales were sluggish. Far from bringing in the $10 million sweepstakes backers had predicted in its first year, the lottery produced only $5.7 million. By 1970, the figure had slipped to $2 million. It was the same dreary story in New York State, where a lottery opened in 1967. There, too, ticket sales declined steadily as the public yawned. Buy a ticket and wait. And wait.

Even if the wait ended in a win, the thrill was less than electrifying. Top prizes in the 1960s were measured in the thousands of dollars. As for the public benefit, that, too, turned out to be disappointing. In 1972, eight years into its operation, the New Hampshire lottery was contributing just $17 per pupil each year to local school systems, hardly enough to raise their performance levels dramatically. By 1972, though, changes were already on the way.

The Excitement Begins

The changes had actually started a couple of years earlier, in 1970, with New Jersey's entry into the lottery business. Officials in that state deliberately set out to plan a game that would be different from either New York's or New Hampshire's—faster-paced and more appealing. New Jersey ticket buyers didn't have to wait up to half a year to find out if they were winners. Drawings were frequent—first weekly, then daily. Business was brisk.

Within months, lottery activity was taking off around the country. States that already had games were revamping them along New Jersey lines. And states without lotteries were getting them. In 1972, Massachusetts and Pennsylvania defied their Puritan and Quaker pasts and hopped on the bandwagon. Massachusetts quickly made lottery history by introducing a new twist—an "instant" game featuring scratch-off tickets that let buyers know at a glance whether they had won or lost. Such instant gratification was apparently exactly what players wanted. The Massachusetts game was wildly popular, and officials in other states soon incorporated variations of it into their own operations. History was made again in 1978, when New York set up its Lotto game and jackpots headed into the millions.

Another lottery milestone was the introduction of computerized betting systems. Computers sped up the games and encouraged players to buy more than one ticket at a time. They also made it possible for ticket buyers to pick their own numbers, and that greater degree of personal participation further heightened excitement. Lottomania was gripping the nation.

By the late 1970s, a total of thirteen states had authorized legal lotteries, and a decade later, the number had more than doubled. In many lottery states, the decision to legalize was made by the citizens at large, rather than through legislation. That's because when the states banned games of chance back in the nineteenth century, a number of them wrote that ban directly into their constitutions. In those states, constitutional changes had to be made before a lottery could be put in place. Changing a constitution in most cases requires a vote in a popular referendum.

Why did lotteries catch on so rapidly in the 1970s and 1980s? Partly because people found them fun to play. There were also the usual money reasons. Although New Hampshire's refusal to consider either a sales tax or an income tax—a refusal that made its lottery venture practically inevitable—was just about unique in the nation, legislators elsewhere were no less eager than those in the Granite State to come up with new ways to increase public revenues. The need to find additional revenue sources became urgent in the mid-1970s because those years marked the start of another period of financial trouble in America.

This time the trouble was a recession—a business slowdown that is serious, but not so much as a full-scale depression. To make matters worse, inflation was also present in the 1970s. During inflation, the price of most everything, from food and fuel to salaries and interest rates, soars. When that happens, governments, like individuals, have a hard time paying their bills. Normally, if lawmakers need extra money, they raise taxes. But people are generally reluctant to pay higher tax bills—and even more reluctant when the cost of everything else is rising, too. A tax laid on the willing only seems especially appropriate during inflation.

Another reason for the rapid movement toward lotteries was that the federal government had backed away from its antilottery position. Congress cooperated in the movement toward state lotteries by approving legislation that allowed lottery advertising in newspapers and magazines sent through the mails. Lawmakers in Washington, D.C., also voted to permit federally chartered banks to handle lottery funds. As we will see in Chapter 4, both banks and advertising are essential to the state lottery business.

Why the federal support for games that produced revenues only on the state level? That's easy. The U.S. government helps fund a number of state-run programs—education and welfare, to name a couple. Anything the states can do to pay for such programs on their own is likely to get backing from Congress and the president.

Yet another reason lotteries spread so quickly is that once one state legalizes a lottery, the pressure is on for other nearby states to do the

same. After New York started its game in 1967, New Jersey citizens, many of whom travel to New York regularly to work or visit, began making a habit of picking up lottery tickets while in the state. That left New Jersey officials watching enviously as *their* taxpayers lined up to pay what was in effect a *New York* State tax. Why should New York be getting New Jersey money? New Jersey lawmakers asked themselves. Their response to the situation was to open a lottery of their own.

It didn't take long for the geographical pattern—and the financial and political demands that produced it—to become clear. From New Hampshire, lotteries spread to other New England states, and by 1974, Vermont alone in the region was without a game. Not until 1978 did the state succumb to lottery pressure.

Other states acted more quickly. Delaware and Maryland, no doubt influenced by Pennsylvania and New Jersey, instituted lotteries in the early seventies. Ohio, Michigan, and Illinois—perhaps also prompted by Pennsylvania—had come to comprise a Midwest lottery cluster by 1974.

More lotteries appeared in the 1980s. The District of Columbia joined the Northeast–Mid-Atlantic group two years into the decade. Meantime, Arizona (1981) and Washington State (1982) opened the door to lottery activity in the West. Colorado, California, and Oregon soon moved in on the action in that part of the country, while in the nation's heartland, Missouri and Iowa began operations in 1985, copied only two years later by Kansas, South Dakota, and Montana. Wisconsin's game got underway in 1988, the same year voters in Minnesota, Idaho, Kentucky, and Indiana approved lottery operations to begin in 1990.

Even in the Southern Bible Belt, long opposed to any form of gambling, lotteries were winning acceptance. West Virginia, which borders on Ohio and Pennsylvania, took the lead in 1986, and by 1988, Florida and Virginia had lotteries as well. Kentucky's game was set to start up two years after that. Altogether, in 1990, 68 percent of the U.S. population could buy official lottery tickets without crossing state lines. But by then, state lotteries represented only part of the country's fast-growing legalized gambling scene.

Super Lotteries

State lotteries never were the only form of legalized gambling open to Americans. In many parts of the country, it's always been possible to "gamble" in various types of private or community lotteries and raffles, for instance. Such games are commonly employed as fund-raisers by Parent-Teacher Associations, volunteer fire departments, hospital support committees, and similar groups. Church bingo is another tradition. The prizes in such contests are small; craft or food items, perhaps, or a few dollars in cash. But the prize is not the point of playing; charity is. Although technically classed as gambling, community raffles and church bingo are hardly the kind of big-time operations most people think of when they hear the word.

But high-stakes operations have also existed—legally— throughout most of U.S. history. Although reformers sought to put an end to all gambling at the time the states outlawed lotteries, legal loopholes permitted some forms of the sport to continue. California, for example, tried to eliminate poker—always particularly popular in that state—by keeping professional dealers from running games. State law did, however, allow nonprofessionals to set up poker parlors and charge players for their use. If those players wanted to bet on a hand, that was their affair. The state of Nevada banned gambling in 1910, but twenty-one years later, in the midst of the Great Depression, the legislature approved a bill legalizing casinos. Since then, cities like Reno and Las Vegas have attracted thousands to their slot machines and roulette tables. Taxes collected on the privately owned and run operations enable the state to avoid enacting an income tax. In some states, horse and dog racing remained legal, and where they did, devotees of the sport could go out to the track and wager on the results. Never, in other words, have Americans lacked the opportunity to gamble legally. Still, before the 1970s, that opportunity was strictly limited.

No more. Not only were state lotteries letting Americans place legal bets in thirty-two states and the District of Columbia, Puerto Rico, and the U.S. Virgin Islands by 1990, but they also had helped pave the way for other types of gambling activities. Among them were regional lotteries.

Regional lotteries might be considered rural America's answer to games like New York's multimillion-dollar Lotto. For New York and other large, populous states, it's relatively easy to get a super game going. Establish the rules, offer tickets for sale, and collect the cash as it comes rolling in. In 1988, all New York lottery operations together brought the state a net income of $725.6 million. (A game's net income is its after-prizes, after-expenses profit. Its gross income is its total proceeds before expenses.) California, also heavily populated and the nation's 1988 lottery profit leader, had a net income of $804 million that year.

For lottery officials in low-population states like Maine or South Dakota, such figures seem an impossible dream. Neither state has enough potential ticket buyers to push jackpots into the millions. What to do? Set up a regional lottery. That's what Maine did in the mid-1980s, joining New Hampshire and Vermont in Tri-State Megabucks. Megabucks officials regard the game as a real winner for the area. In their individual state lotteries, Maine and New Hampshire were each taking in gross proceeds of about $60 million by the late 1980s. Vermont was taking in $25 million. At the same time, Megabucks was grossing over $82 million annually. An even broader regional operation is Lotto America, founded jointly under a 1987 compact among Iowa, Kansas, Oregon, Rhode Island, West Virginia, and the District of Columbia. Other states have since joined the game and some experts in the field expect it to form the nucleus of an eventual national lottery.

Another gambling trend in the United States today: games sponsored by members of Native American tribal organizations. By 1989, gambling operations were being conducted at 120 of the 310 reservations in the contiguous forty-eight states.

Native Americans are attracted to lottery operations for the same reason other citizens are: They are a tax people want to pay. And those who want to do the paying in this case are not so much the Native Americans who live on the reservations as the outsiders who show up on game nights. The Creek Nation of Oklahoma, which opened a bingo game in 1984, draws 50,000 players a year, nearly all of them white. Of the more than $22 million those players spend yearly, the Creeks get to keep about $3 million. Other bingo games are held at the Chitimacha Indian Reservation in Louisiana. According to *Time* magazine, every Saturday night 1,200 people pay a $45 admission charge there to take a chance on Chitimacha prizes that start at $1,000 for each winning card.

Native American gaming operations have been helped along by the fact that, under U.S. law, the tribes enjoy special sovereign status, meaning each can run its game largely free of state supervision. In the fall of 1988, Congress gave the tribal gambling business another boost with a law freeing it to move beyond bingo into more sophisticated types of play. Under the new law, reservation leaders may petition a state to conduct any type of gambling activity that is legal within that state—casino games or betting on horse and dog races, for example. Another law, one that took effect in 1990, permits the tribes to advertise such activities nationally.

National advertising may help the Native American games—but the games may be hurt by the fact that they will be getting more and more competition from the states. As the 1990s dawned, the states seemed to be holding a contest to see which could most quickly legalize the greatest variety of gambling activities.

Beyond Lotteries

The first state to move beyond lotteries was New York with its 1971 introduction of the Offtrack Betting (OTB) Corporation. OTB allowed racing enthusiasts to place their wagers without having to go out to the racecourse. All they had to do was walk into a neighborhood OTB shop. The state, of course, taxes OTB proceeds. By 1990, offtrack betting was legal in Connecticut and Nevada as well.

The rush to move beyond lotteries picked up speed in 1976, when New Jersey voters got to decide whether or not to permit casino gambling in the rundown old resort of Atlantic City. Backers of the idea hammered away at two basic themes. Taxing the casinos would help the state keep individual taxes low, and the industry would mean new building and new life for the dilapidated town. New Jersey was persuaded, and Atlantic City became a sort of Las Vegas–East. At the time, it was the only place outside of Nevada with casinos in the United States. Since then, Puerto Rico has welcomed casino gambling and so has Deadwood, South Dakota. Deadwood, once home to the legendary gambler "Wild Bill" Hickok, hoped to capitalize on its gaudy past by pulling in gamesters and tourists from all across America. South Dakota's casinos opened in 1989, the same year Iowa authorized a 1991 start to casino gambling on old-fashioned riverboats on the Mississippi.

If any state provides a measure of America's growing devotion to gambling, it is Iowa. As recently as 1983, even church bingo games were illegal in the state. Six years later, not only was bingo legal and riverboat gambling on its way, but Iowans could also buy tickets in a state lottery and in Lotto America. They could gamble in card rooms and place bets at four separate racetracks. If they wanted, they could gamble right in their own living rooms, thanks to a television program produced by state lottery officials and involving contestants in the studio and viewers at home. The TV show was a smash hit around the state, outdrawing even the ever-popular "Wheel of Fortune."

But Iowa is not the only state coming up with more and more gambling innovations. In South Dakota, people can gamble on video devices—what a writer for *Business Week* magazine called "electronic near-equivalents of slot machines"—in bars and other places of business. Betting on professional sports, once strictly against the law, appears to be another wave of the future. The state of Oregon began a football betting scheme in 1989. Sports betting is also legal in Nevada and has come up for serious discussion in Massachusetts, Connecticut, New Hampshire, and Kentucky. In only two states, Hawaii and Utah, was gambling of any kind absolutely against the law as the 1990s began.

Legalized gambling is more than big in the United States today—it is big business. All in all, Americans wagered a legal $210.8 billion in 1988, and the industry's after-expenses profits amounted to $21.3 billion. Those figures were enough to put legalized gambling in thirteenth place in the *Forbes* list of the nation's 500 top moneymaking businesses. They also made legalized gambling the number-one growth industry in the country.

Most people expect the growth to continue and for a number of reasons. There are all the old ones, of course. Most Americans still think of gambling as a harmless amusement. And in many eyes, it remains an appealing tax substitute, one that will be increasingly in demand if the country's budget crunch worsens. So far, worsening is exactly what it has been doing. At the beginning of the 1980s, the U.S. national debt was an enormous $1 trillion. By the decade's end, that figure had tripled. Yet despite the shortfall, President George Bush had promised that his administration would ask Congress for no new taxes. He seemed determined to keep that promise, and in fact, was pushing for a reduction in the capital gains tax, the levy placed on certain business and stock market deals. In October, 1990, however, Bush did agree to slightly higher taxes on the wealthiest Americans, as well as increases in federal taxes on gasoline, beer, cigarettes, and certain luxuries. Most state and local officials were as reluctant as the president to raise taxes.

But how could politicians get away with not raising taxes? Americans were demanding more and more services from government at all levels: better schools, an effective war on illegal drugs, action to help the nation's hundreds of thousands of homeless, affordable health care . . . the list went on and on. The 1991 Persian Gulf War drained more billions from the U.S. Treasury. To many in and out of government, increasing gambling activity—and taxing gambling proceeds in one way or another—seemed to be the only acceptable means of raising money for a multitude of public purposes.

There are other, newer reasons gambling activity may increase in the coming years. People in many towns and cities—Atlantic City, New Jersey, is one and Deadwood, South Dakota, another—see conversion to a gaming center as a quick and easy way to revitalize old downtowns. Another impetus toward gambling comes from the fact that a considerable percentage of the U.S. population has the spare time—and cash—to indulge in it. Although homelessness and poverty were a fact of life for record numbers of U.S. families in the late 1980s, the decade saw upper-income Americans becoming more affluent, not less. Another factor likely to stimulate gambling is the rise in the population of elderly Americans. During the 1980s, the number of men and women aged sixty-five and over went up 18.9 percent. Gambling is especially popular with people in that age group, and buses headed for Las Vegas and Atlantic City are typically filled with "senior citizens."

Nor is state-sponsored gambling the only type that's on the rise in the United States today. Illegal gambling is becoming more widespread as well, and some say that today, as in the past, there is a connection between it and the legalized variety. We will look more closely at that claim in Chapter 5. What's more, in a revival of a trend that began with the commercial expansion of sixteenth century Europe, lotteries are proliferating as business promotions. Magazine companies routinely use sweepstakes contests as a means of encouraging new subscriptions, for example. What American is not familiar with television personality Ed McMahon's yearly exhortations to grab at the chance of millions of dollars "all for *you?*" Supermarkets seek to attract customers by advertising weekly drawings for prizes that range from trips to Disneyland to color television sets to free groceries. At least two major U.S. credit card companies have held lotteries in which cardholders were automatically entered every time they charged a purchase. Open a package of chicken, and out falls a plastic-wrapped sweepstakes ticket. A similar ticket is to be found in a bag of English muffins. A battery-operated watch, which breaks down after a month, incidentally, comes with every twenty-fifth box of garbage bags. Even the U.S. Postal Service has gotten into the lottery act. To publicize its October 1989 issue of four dinosaur stamps, the post office announced a Win-the-Adventure-of-a-Lifetime random drawing—grand prize, a five-day trip to Dinosaur National Park on the Colorado/Utah border.

Truly, America has become the land of lotteries.

4

"Imagine the Feeling..."

On Wednesday, November 15, 1989, twenty-three-year-old Anhtinh Ton Giang won $6 million in Ohio's Super Lotto game. Although not outstandingly large by 1989 standards, the win nevertheless made headlines around the country. Anhtinh Ton Giang's story was the kind people love to read and hear about, a classic American success story—1980s style—and one certain to warm the heart of even the severest of lottery critics.

When Anhtinh was born in the Southeast Asian nation of South Vietnam, that country was at war. The struggle was between the government of South Vietnam and South Vietnamese rebels, aided by the communist government of neighboring North Vietnam. The South's weak, unpopular regime was supported by the United States. By the time Anhtinh was two, nearly half a million Americans were on combat duty in Vietnam. About 60,000 of them died in the course of the fighting. So did 200,000 South Vietnamese soldiers and more than a million civilians. Many of the civilian dead were the accidental victims of U.S. guns and bombs. But the harder this country fought to keep South Vietnam from going communist, the more determined the rebels and their North Vietnamese allies seemed to become, and before

Anhtinh was ten, they had their victory. Vietnam was a single communist nation.

For the boy, peace brought no respite. The Giangs had been loyal to the South Vietnamese government and to its American backers, and anti-U.S. feeling was high in the aftermath of the fighting. The Giangs and others like them faced official persecution, and Anhtinh eventually fled the country. His brother Cam, an uncle, and a cousin managed to get out, too. The rest of the family remained in Vietnam. "It was very tough," Anhtinh said later. He spent a year and a half in a refugee camp in Indonesia, and at age eighteen, a resettlement agency sent him to Columbus, Ohio.

"I was very poor," the young man recalled, "but I always worked hard." His job: stitching interior auto trim for a salary of $5.75 an hour. It was a job he quit the day after his $6 million windfall. But in the best American tradition of hard work and determination to get ahead, Anhtinh scoffed at the notion of living off his lottery earnings, $240,000 a year for twenty years. "I'm not [the kind of] person to get a lot of money and sit around," he told reporters. "I'd like to do work that would improve myself." Starting up a construction business and remodeling old houses was one possibility, he added. He also planned to pay Cam's way through Ohio State University.

Anhtinh's story captured the imagination of Americans. It had all the elements of a fairy tale: deprived childhood, wicked villains, and wandering hero; the struggle to survive, the kindness of strangers—and the final, sudden glorious turn of fortune with its promise of a happily-ever-after ending. And it had, as well, that special American flavor. Anhtinh's experience seemed proof that the old frontier is not dead, that a poor boy can still make good if he's willing to pioneer, to gamble, to stake everything on the small chance of winning. It was proof, if proof were needed, that anyone, anyone at all, can do the same. Who wouldn't buy an extra lottery ticket or two after hearing about Anhtinh?

Anyone with common sense, some people would say. Lottery winners like Anhtinh may get a lot of publicity, but they're extremely rare—one or two in millions. Anyone hoping to make good in life should stay away from state lottery machines and save the cost of a ticket, critics say. Why? Because lotteries are designed to make money, not give it away. Their purpose is to produce losers, not winners. The critics add that anyone who bothered to read up on lotteries and find out how they work—instead of focusing on exceptions like Antinh—would know that perfectly well.

Lottery Organization

When the states began reinstituting lotteries in the 1960s, they had a choice of how to organize them. The first possibility was to place the games in the hands of private business. That would mean licensing a company to set up the lottery, run it, and return a fixed percentage of the proceeds to the state. This is the way in which the nation's legal gambling casinos are organized. They are owned and directed by private corporations licensed and taxed by the state. Ontrack betting in the United States is also generally managed by state-licensed private owners.

There are advantages to allowing the private ownership of gaming operations. Private companies are usually more flexible than government agencies. They can deal with employees free of the civil service rules that restrict hiring and firing in the public sector, for instance, and adapt their procedures as needed in response to changing circumstances. Because private enterprise pursues the profit motive, it would have every reason to try to maximize lottery profits, and that could be an important consideration for states looking for every penny they can get in new revenues. Above all, in the view of many, private licensing lets a government benefit from a lottery while not putting it in the position of urging its own citizens to gamble away their hard-earned dollars.

But as state lawmakers saw matters, the disadvantages of instituting lotteries as privately run businesses outweighed the advantages. Chief among the former was the threat of corruption. It was private brokers and contractors whose tolerance of fraud had helped bring about the banning of lotteries in the previous century. Modern state officials knew that keeping the games honest must be a number-one priority if they were to succeed as fund-raisers. Keeping them free of political manipulation would be a priority, too, and such manipulation is more likely in a private system than in one open to public scrutiny. The Louisiana lottery experience provided ample evidence of that fact.

Having dismissed the idea of privately administered lotteries, state officials moved on to consider a second possibility: establishing public benefit corporations to do the administering. This relatively new type of corporation is a public-private amalgam, run along the lines of a private business but with directors appointed by the government. Profits are returned, not to the corporation, but to state tax authorities. New York's Offtrack Betting (OTB) is an example of a gaming operation controlled by a public benefit corporation.

The pluses of assigning lotteries to public benefit corporation management are obvious. Such a corporation will be able to operate with more flexibility than a government agency. At the same time, it will be subject to greater government regulation than the average private company.

Not subject enough, though, state officials decided. Again, thoughts of the Louisiana lottery—itself run through a setup resembling a public benefit corporation—deterred them. And so, as state after state adopted a game, each one settled on the third organizational possibility: public ownership and control.

Public ownership and control with an assist from private enterprise, that is. Although details vary slightly among the states, the basic lottery format is for a publicly appointed lottery commission to provide administration and direction, with ticket sales and distribution left up to private businesses. The commission, along with the lottery director and its deputy directors, directs production and promotion, while designated banks hold lottery funds. Banks also hold lottery tickets and distribute them for sale in such commercial outlets as grocery and convenience stores. The owners of these outlets thus become lottery sales agents and receive a commission on ticket sales. Commissions range from 4.1 percent in Massachusetts to 12.1 percent in Iowa. Nationwide, they average 5.5 percent. In addition to the regular commission, the owner of a business that chances to sell a winning ticket may get a substantial bonus. Other private business owners may profit, too. State lottery officials contract with companies to design the games and to provide the needed equipment, including lottery computer terminals. Among the nation's leading lottery contractors have been Bally Manufacturing of Chicago and its Georgia subsidiary, Scientific Games; Minnesota's Control Data Corporation; and the Rhode Island-based Gtech Corporation.

Lottery commissions are constructed, and their members appointed, in slightly different ways, according to each state's rules. A commission may be independent, or it may be part of a state bureau of taxation. Members may be named to their posts by the governor, or by the governor and legislature together. The responsibility for day-to-day lottery operations belongs to the lottery director, who, under the particular setup, gets a greater or lesser degree of input from the commission. Acting under the director are a number of deputy directors who deal with accounting, licensing, security, personnel, ticket manufacturing, promotion, and the all-important drawings and validation of winners.

Lotteries operate differently today than they did when New Hampshire opened its sweepstakes in 1964. To enter that state's game, or the New York lottery that began three years later, a person bought a ticket, wrote his or her name and address in the space provided, tore off a receipt, and returned the ticket to the sales agent. Tickets collected from around the state were placed in a container to be mixed up together. Finally, weeks or months later, came the drawing. Lottery officials present at this event would know immediately who the winner was—his or her name and address would be right on the ticket. They would notify the lucky individual, who would produce the saved receipt, and the game would start over with new tickets and new sales.

Lotteries don't work like that anymore. When New Jersey officials introduced their weekly, then daily, drawings at the start of the 1970s, they did more than speed things up. They moved to a different type of game altogether, one that quickly became the model for the nation.

The New Jersey Model

The New Jersey game is based on numbers rather than names. Players buy tickets, each of which bears a number or numbers. In a majority of games, players can choose between picking the number or numbers themselves or having the computer do it for them. Once purchased, tickets are neither collected nor mixed. Nor is one drawn to determine the winner. Instead, a drum is filled with numbered balls, and it is these that are tumbled together before several are selected at random. Depending upon the type of game being played, three, four, five, or six balls may be drawn. The numbers on the balls become the winning combination, which is immediately publicized through the news media. Players simply listen to radio or TV or check the newspaper and compare the winning number to the number or numbers on their ticket. Since lottery officials have no way of knowing who the winner is, it's up to that individual to appear at lottery headquarters to claim the prize. Computerized records do, however, tell state authorities the name of the outlet at which the ticket was purchased, and those records ensure that the correct sales agent gets any bonus.

The fact that modern state lotteries are based on an individually picked number or numbers explains why the games so often produce multiple winners like the four who shared more than $20 million in Illinois in September 1988. A game that involves the drawing of a single name will naturally have only one winner. So will a number-based game in which tickets are preprinted, with each number being used only once. But when players choose their own numbers, duplication is likely. It is especially likely if the number drawn happens to relate to a news event or something else that has caught the public's attention. For example, says Bill Adler, author of *The Lottery Book,* "After the hijacking of TWA flight 847 to Beirut," which happened on June 14, 1985, and resulted in the death of one American on board, "lottery players around the country bet heavily on the digits 847." Massachusetts bets placed on those numbers in the wake of the terrorist incident were ten times higher than average. If the numbers had turned up in the drawing, there would have been an extraordinarily large group of winners. Of course, each would have received only a portion of the total prize. When Billy Martin, former manager of baseball's New York Yankees, was killed in a 1989 auto accident, New York lottery officials had to suspend play on the numbers 3569. The reason: too many players had bet on Martin's license plate number, VR3569.

Not only did the New Jersey system make lotteries easier and more exciting to play, but it also allowed for the faster sale of tickets, and that pleased state officials eager to make as many sales as they could as quickly as they could. The system offered an advantage to players, too, eliminating any possibility that their tickets might be misplaced or destroyed and guaranteeing their entry in the contest. That advantage worked to the states' advantage as well. Public confidence is an essential ingredient in any successful lottery. If people cannot trust a game, they will not play it. It is largely because people believe state lotteries are honestly and efficiently run that the games are as effective as they have been at raising money.

Behind-the-scenes lottery operations are similarly aimed at

ensuring public trust. Winning tickets are returned to lottery headquarters to be checked against prizes paid out. Careful financial records are kept and audited twice to guard against cheating. Security regarding the manufacture and distribution of tickets is tight. Because banks are generally regarded as sound institutions accustomed to dealing honestly with large sums of money, they have been the ones chosen to handle lottery funds and distribute tickets. We saw in Chapter 3 that the U.S. Congress helped the lottery business along with a law permitting federally chartered banks to participate in the state schemes.

Despite all the precautions, though, questions about lottery integrity do crop up from time to time. The director of the Maine lottery resigned in 1985 after it became known that he had broken state rules by entertaining lottery sales agents and their families. He had also, again contrary to the rules, accepted free services from the game's principal contractor, Scientific Games. Four years later, fraud charges were filed against two Pennsylvania men alleged to have used a computer to forge a winning ticket worth $15 million. In another Pennsylvania incident, some lottery officials were found to have injected liquid latex into most of the numbered balls used in the drawing. The latex made the balls heavier, and that meant that the untreated balls—those marked with the numbers on which the officials had bet—rose to the top of the hopper and were picked. The fraud was discovered in 1980, before those who had concocted it could collect their "winnings." Each spent between two and five years in prison. In Tennessee, which does not have a state lottery but which does permit charitable bingo, bribery and corruption charges have been leveled against two dozen people allegedly involved in cash-skimming schemes. Two state officials caught up in the investigation committed suicide.

Winning Players

Keeping their games honest is not the only challenge for lottery officials. Another is getting people to play them, not once or twice, but over and over again. If people don't play, jackpot levels won't keep growing. That would mean disaster, the officials believe. Their research indicates that it's those ever-rising prizes that attract players to a game. "People play . . . to get rich," says the marketing director for one state lottery. Let prizes level off—or worse, shrink—and players will find other ways to spend their money. Upward-spiraling prizes will become downward-spiraling ones, and lotteries will fail as a source of state revenue. To keep that from happening and to make sure players keep coming back, lottery officials depend upon constant innovation: introducing twists and gimmicks in the rules; varying the prizes; coming up with new ways to win; tinkering with the odds; increasing promotion; promising more speed, more action, more choice, more excitement, more everything.

So the lottery scene grows increasingly frenetic. Twice-a-year games become weekly contests, then daily and instant ones. Then they turn into games that aren't really over even when they seem to be, games in which losing tickets may be automatically entered in a secondary game with a renewed chance of winning.

The innovations seem unending. New games appear. During the fall-winter National Football League season, lottery officials may be pushing a game with a football motif; come spring, the theme switches to baseball. "We do Olympics," Oregon's lottery director said in 1989. "At Christmas we do Holiday Cash. With Lucky Stars we play on people's astrological signs." In 1990, Maine lottery officials sought to capitalize on one of the state's natural resources by introducing a "Moose on the Loose" game. In many instances, contests with differing themes run simultaneously because, as the Oregon lottery director says, "We find that if you run two or three, four or five games at the same time, you'll sell more tickets."

Running simultaneous games is not the only trick of the trade. Prize offerings are doubled, redoubled. In a state where the chance of winning a multimillion-dollar jackpot is only one in four million, the chance of winning a free new ticket in an instant game may be as high as one in eight or nine. "People want to see winners," according to one lottery director. "We set up the prize structure so we have a lot of winners in the store. It's not a mathematical formula, it's a human relations formula."

Lottery officials strive to "humanize" their contests in other ways. In New Jersey, instant tickets began coming in three different colors. The idea caught on quickly. "People say, 'that's different,' " says lottery director Barbara Marrow. " 'That must be something new.' " In every state, players are urged to throw themselves into the spirit of the game, to use birthdates and other personal anniversaries to determine their own special number combinations, or to fantasize about what to do with their earnings. Ticket machines are no longer limited to grocery store locations. They've spread to card shops, gas stations, liquor stores, video outlets, even, according to *Forbes* magazine, to funeral parlors. They are also more likely and more to be found in "idle time" places like airports, where bored people wander around looking for something to do.

Increasingly, what people—bored or otherwise—are finding to do is to gamble. This fact may delight state lottery officials, who are congratulating themselves on having created structures and operations that generate billions in proceeds every year. But the fact that lotteries attract so many—half of the U.S. population had played in a state game at one time or another by 1989—troubles some Americans. One of the things they find most disturbing is the way state lottery officials advertise their games.

In the beginning, lottery advertising was minimal. When New

Hampshire started its sweepstakes, state officials made an effort to keep the venture low key. They announced the existence of the game and made tickets available. Towns and cities had the option of deciding whether or not to permit sales within their confines. Where ticket sales were okayed, signs were displayed.

Other states were even more cautious in their early years of lottery operation. When Missouri initiated its game in 1985, advertising was forbidden altogether. For a while, the lottery limped along, with actual proceeds falling well short of earlier projections. Eventually, state lawmakers overturned the advertising ban, at the same time killing a rule that limited the amount lottery officials could spend on operating costs. Profits shot up. Missouri people had discovered that to succeed, a state lottery must be promoted.

New Hampshire people learned the same lesson. By the 1970s, sweepstakes advertising had intensified. In other lottery states, too, more and more ads were appearing in newspapers, on billboards, and throughout public transit systems. Acting under pressure from the states, Congress legalized broadcast ads for lotteries. By the mid-1980s, according to the Television Bureau of Advertising, states were putting $23.3 million a year into TV ads. Five years later, twenty-eight states and the District of Columbia were spending more than four times that amount on lottery advertising in all the media. Much of that money, lottery critics maintain, pays for ads that are misleading—or downright dishonest.

Truth in Advertising?

Advertising in the United States is not supposed to be dishonest. Sure, ads hype products: this toothpaste means a date to the prom; that spaghetti sauce wins the family's love; the right brand of medicine has cold sufferers on their way in minutes. But there are rules aimed at keeping the assertions within reasonable bounds. An ad for aspirin, for example, may say that the product relieves cold symptoms, but may not include the claim that it kills the virus. The Federal Trade Commission (FTC) is the government agency charged with the primary responsibility for ensuring truth in advertising.

But the FTC has no jurisdiction over state lottery advertising—or over state advertising for other types of legalized gambling. The agency's power of enforcement is limited to private enterprise. "It may disapprove, but it can't touch fraud by state governments," Eliot Marshall, former senior editor of *The New Republic* magazine, has complained. It, or some other agency, ought to be able to, he and others believe. "It offends the . . . sense of decency that anyone should openly peddle a product so clearly designed to seduce the gullible," Marshall wrote. "Lotteries are in the business of selling illusions."

Illusions? Seduce? Fraud? Yes, the critics say. What else is it but fraud when a lottery ad depicts players demonstrating the "right" way to rub a scratch-off ticket to make sure of winning? There is *no* right way. Winning in an honest lottery is a matter of random chance and nothing else. Yet lottery ads also feature people discussing their "systems" for coming up with sure-fire winning number combinations. Absolutely no such system exists. For lottery officials to imply that one does is as false as for aspirin makers to say that they have a cure for the common cold—a statement that would have the FTC knocking at their doors within hours. That's what the critics contend, anyway.

Lottery ads are misleading, or worse, in more ways than one, the critics go on. The ads make it sound as if winning happened all the time. It doesn't. What is more, many who do count as winners get no more than a dollar or two or perhaps an extra ticket. But in ads, even these "winners" seem as thrilled as the latest lottery millionaire. Other ads urge people to think about—even to plan—how to spend their prize money. Always, there's the assumption that not only will the prize be won, but also that it will be "the big one." The theme of a 1989 series of ads for the Maine State lottery: "Just imagine the feeling." In New York, ads encouraged players to explore their wildest dreams: "Instead of waiting for a bus, I'd have a limo waiting for me," says one young woman. For that woman, and for everyone else who plays a state lottery, it is extremely unlikely that the dream will ever be more than a mirage.

Other ads for state-sponsored gambling operations similarly deal in illusion. "Everybody Loves a Winner," a New York OTB subway ad stated in bold typeface. The illustration showed a man in formal dress surrounded by seven other rich-looking people. The clear implication: "Everybody *Is* a Winner." Advertising copywriters for the Illinois State lottery didn't stop with implications. "Money Does Grow on Trees," was one slogan they came up with. According to *The Christian Science Monitor*, an ad for the Washington, D.C., lottery drew a comparison between the game and civil rights leader Martin Luther King, Jr.'s dream of racial and economic justice for Americans of all races. That ad, aimed at a largely black and relatively poor population, struck many observers as especially offensive.

Odds Against . . .

Another complaint about lottery ads is that they are deceptive about the odds of winning. Maine lottery officials claim that the chance of winning their instant game is "typically" one in four, but the chances of winning the game's top prize are a far, far longer one in 12,000. The ads ignore that statistic. They also gloss over the fact that the top instant game prize is $1,000; nice, but not exactly in the millions. The chances of winning Maine's Tri-State Megabucks are one in 3.8 million. Elsewhere, the odds are worse. Nationally, only 0.000008 percent of the 97 million lottery tickets sold in 1988 turned out to be worth $1 million or more to their buyers.

What do such appallingly bad odds mean to individual players? Jean Lemaire, professor of mathematics at the University of Pennsylvania's Wharton School of Business and a specialist in figuring odds, offered an explanation. In 1989, as people were lining up to buy chances on Pennsylvania's $115 million jackpot, Lemaire calculated that the chances of being the single winner of that prize were less than the chances of playing eighty-eight rounds of Russian roulette (one chamber of a revolver out of six holding a bullet) and surviving. Winning would also be less likely than living past the age of 115. "Or, in other words," he concluded, "if all 102 settlers on the *Mayflower* had purchased a lottery ticket once a week" (unlikely behavior among that group of Puritans) "and given instructions to their descendants to continue until today—there are eighty chances out of a hundred that no one would have won." In fact, Professor Lemaire's point was well taken; there was no single winner of Pennsylvania's mammoth jackpot. The prize ended up being split fourteen ways. But lottery ads don't have much to say about shared prizes.

Lottery advertising is also quiet about the fact that state lottery commissions deliberately make their prizes harder and harder to claim by repeatedly lengthening the odds against winning. When a man named Lou Eisenberg won $5 million in New York's Lotto in 1981, he did so by overcoming odds of close to two million to one. Seven years later, Eisenberg was obliging the state commission by taping ads for the game—but without mentioning the fact that the odds he beat had been changed to almost 13 million to one. How had the change come about? In 1981, a lotto winner had to pick six correct numbers out of a total of forty. "Lotto 40 became Lotto 44 in October 1983," Zachary M. Berman of Brooklyn pointed out in a 1988 letter to *The New York Times*, meaning that the six matching numbers had to be chosen from a field of forty-four. "Lotto 44 became Lotto 48 in June 1985," he continued. "This year, Lotto 48 begat Lotto 54." To win at that game, a person would have to get six figures right out of fifty-four—"insurmountable" odds, Berman called them. Perhaps they are. If so, they were meant to be. As we saw earlier in this chapter, lotteries are designed to produce losers, not winners. We also saw the reason for that: Big jackpots bring in big proceeds. The simplest way to raise jackpots is to make the odds of claiming one so bad that it "rolls over" winnerless week after week, snowballing as it goes.

Also making state lotteries tough to win is the fact that most pay out only half or less of their proceeds in prizes. Exceptions in 1988 were Illinois, Connecticut, Iowa, and Wisconsin, each of which paid out 51 percent to winners, as well as Vermont (52 percent); Delaware (53 percent); and Massachusetts (a whopping 59 percent). Kansas, the least generous of states, was giving away just 44 percent of gross revenues that year. A racetrack operation, by contrast, returns 80 percent of its take to bettors, and at casino slot machines and roulette tables, payout rates may be as high as 95 percent. Even illegal numbers games return 60 percent to those who play them, a fact it is certain no one will learn about from lottery ads.

How Much Money Do Prizewinners Really Get?

Another fraudulent element in lottery advertising, according to the critics, is that the ads fail to make clear how much winners really get. In the first place, the ads tend to ignore the tax bite. The "$6 million" Anhtinh Ton Giang won in 1989, for instance, boils down to $4.8 million after taxes. Of course that is not the advertiser's fault, nor the lottery commission's. State and federal governments insist upon taking their share of lottery jackpots. It's different in Canada, by the way. In that country, lottery winnings are not taxed.

But even though U.S. lottery officials do not set tax policy, they are the ones responsible for the fact that Anhtinh will get his $4.8 million, not in one lump sum, but as twenty annual installments. Not that nearly a quarter of a million dollars a year for twenty years is anything to sneeze at, but it is not as much—and the ads utterly ignore this aspect of lottery operation—as Anhtinh would have had if Ohio had given him his entire winnings upfront. Wisely invested over twenty years, the money would have grown to considerably more than $4.8 million.

Beyond that, the amount of money a state pays out in megaprizes comes to much less even than a winner's after-tax earnings. That is because rather than setting aside the entire amount of a prize, a state buys annuity policies for its big winners. Each annuity, plus the interest it earns, becomes the prize.

How much can a state save with annuities? Sheelah Ryan won "$55 million" in a 1988 Florida lottery, but the state paid only $26 million for her policy. She will get the money owed her, but less than half of it will come from actual lottery proceeds. If, on the other hand, she had gotten the full $55 million and bought her own annuity, she might have ended with twice that amount.

The Media Connection

Besides the paid lottery advertising that appears throughout the U.S. media, state lottery operations benefit from a considerable amount of free advertising. This comes in the form of breathless headlines about mounting jackpots—"Big Jackpot, Big Dollars, Big Dreams," *The New York Times* cried as a 1990 pot grew to $35 million—and glowing articles about such appealing winners as Anhtinh Ton Giang. Other media stories seem to express admiration for the willingness of some lottery players to make serious financial sacrifices. "I'd better win, because this is the mortgage money!" one ticket buyer in Pennsylvania's $115 million game was quoted as saying.

Financial adviser and columnist Sylvia Porter deplores the use of quotes like that one. "Lionizing such behavior makes little sense," she says. "Fiscal irresponsibility is not heroic." Writing in *The Christian Century*, Byron L. Rohrig hints at one reason reporters, editors, and news managers are so eager to provide free lottery publicity. Because of the lottery advertising media outlets are paid to carry, Rohrig contends, those outlets "have vested interests in state lotteries."

Sometimes the interest lands a news organization in trouble. On January 7, 1990, the day after the drawing in New York's $35 million game, the only fact reporters knew for sure about the outcome was that one ticket holder had walked away with the entire amount. Not until ten o'clock that night did the city's WWOR-TV, Channel 9, manage to break the news: The winner was an unmarried Dobbs Ferry woman named Charlie Taylor. Channel 4, WNBC-TV, carried the Taylor story on its 11 P.M. broadcast, and next morning's *New York Post* blared: "$35M AND SHE'S SINGLE!" But it was the *Post*'s rival, *The New York Daily News*, that came up with the real scoop. "IT'S A HOAX," the *News* screamed, and its editors were right. A prankster, Alan Abel, aided by a professional actress and several others, had succeeded in duping the staffs at the *Post* and the two television stations. The actual winner of the $35 million prize was a man, a middle-aged automobile mechanic.

Lottery commissions take no responsibility for hoaxes like Abel's. In fact, New York commissioners may have been pleased by the publicity his action engendered. But lottery officials and the outside agencies they hire to run their advertising campaigns do take issue with the criticisms aimed in their direction. They object to the idea that they ought to be informing consumers about the drawbacks of delayed payments, low payout rates, the odds against winning, and so on. Their objection is based on the feeling that they are not so much selling the chance of winning as they are selling the dream of winning. The chance of walking off with millions may be infinitesimal, but the dream belongs to everyone. "It's just as much fun to think about winning as it is to win," one lottery promoter says. And it costs only $1.

Only $1. That amount buys a big dream—and a tiny chance of that dream coming true, lottery defenders say. But that is not all it buys. In states like New York, New Hampshire, and Montana, it buys better education for children. In Pennsylvania, it buys health care for the elderly. In Arizona, it helps pay for transportation systems, and in

67

Colorado it provides parks and recreational facilities. In all thirty-two states, and in the District of Columbia, Puerto Rico, and the U.S. Virgin Islands, $1 buys freedom from more direct forms of taxation. "Everybody wins," Wallace G. Soule, Jr., director of the Maine lottery, says of the game in his state. "I don't see as there are any losers."

His words echo those that advertised the 1777 lottery intended to raise funds for General George Washington's army: "Even the unsuccessful adventurer will have the pleasing reflection of having contributed a degree to the great and glorious American cause." And they recall the ballad in praise of the Virginia Company's Jamestown lottery: "Let no man thinke that he shall loose, though he no Prize poscesse . . ."

Only $1—and there are no losers. Everyone wins. Or do they?

5

"Real and Substantiall Food?"

One trillion, one hundred and ninety-four billion, five hundred million dollars. That's how much Americans paid in federal, state, and local taxes in 1986. It's a huge amount of money—$1,194.5 trillion. The figure looks even larger when you compare it to tax collections in other nations. The British, for example, paid just $213.6 billion in taxes in 1986. Canadians paid $123.8 billion. In Sweden, the bill came to $70.2 billion, and in next-door Norway, to less than half that, $34.8 billion.

Is that why American taxpayers are feeling fed up and overburdened? Is that why politicians are happy to see lotteries, OTB, and other forms of legalized gambling substituting for new tax laws? Politicians know that if they want to be reelected to office, they must please the public, something more easily done by lowering taxes than by raising them. Lawmakers reckon that the longer they can keep lottery revenues flowing—and new tax laws off the books—the safer their jobs are.

That kind of reckoning may be good politics, but is it good tax policy? Some Americans think not. Not only do lotteries and similar operations constitute a type of tax, the critics point out, but they constitute an inherently unfair and regressive one.

A Regressive Tax?

A tax may be either regressive or progressive. A progressive tax requires the rich to pay proportionately more than the poor. The U.S. federal income tax is a moderately progressive tax, since people with incomes over a certain level are taxed at a higher rate than the less well off. In 1990, a married couple filing a joint tax statement and earning under $32,450 a year paid federal income tax at the rate of 15 percent. Couples earning more than that amount paid a 28 percent tax.

A regressive tax, on the other hand, is the same for everyone. People who live in a state with a 5 percent sales tax pay that 5 percent regardless of income. If a millionaire buys a $4 movie ticket, he pays a 20-cent tax on it. The $200 a week janitor who is next at the box office pays the same. So do the unemployed waiter, the college student, and the doctor who follow them in line. Everyone pays equally.

Except that it isn't really equal. Five percent of $4 is a small amount, and the waiter and college student may not miss the 20 cents much more than the doctor or the millionaire will. But when the same charge is repeated over and over, on purchases ranging from clothing and cars to over-the-counter medicines and restaurant meals, it mounts up. And the sum total takes a bigger bite out of a working class salary than it does out of a doctor's income or a millionaire's inherited wealth.

Lotteries, too, their critics say, take more from the poor than from the rich. According to some studies, a disproportionate number of lottery players live at the lower end of the income scale. A report released by the National Bureau of Economic Research shows affluent Americans spending a smaller share of their income on lottery tickets than needier ones. Why the difference? Many experts in the field think it reflects the fact that the desire to gamble is a natural human instinct, one that the prosperous can satisfy without having recourse to a state lottery.

"The middle classes and the rich don't usually gamble through lotteries," says Gary S. Becker, professor of economics and sociology at the University of Chicago. They do their risk-taking elsewhere, in the world of high finance, for instance. Not for them the fun of buying a $1 instant lottery ticket and the ritual of scratching it "just so" to see whether they've won. Their thrills come from pouring hundreds, thousands, even millions, of dollars into the stock market, buying and selling company shares, bonds, and so on. Less-well-off Americans don't have that option. State lotteries, ontrack and offtrack betting, and legalized games at places like casinos and poker parlors are the only lawful forms of gambling in which they can afford to indulge.

It's an expensive indulgence. As we saw in Chapter 4, lotteries are designed to take away more than they give back. In most lottery states, half or less of gross proceeds are returned in prizes. An average of about 15 percent goes to pay for operating expenses, including commissions and bonuses; in 1988, New York, New Jersey, and Maryland spent the smallest percentage of proceeds—9 percent—to run their games. Kansas spent the greatest, 36 percent. Amounts going to state departments of revenue that year ranged from a high of 44 percent in New York and Missouri to a low of 20 percent in Kansas. Add the state's share to its operating costs, and the result is a hefty tax—53 cents on each $1 lottery ticket in New York, for example. In Kansas, it's 56 cents. Fifty-three or 56 percent is an enormous rate for a tax.

Business tax rates are nowhere near as high. Writing in the magazine *Business Week*, Professor Becker pointed to the "low tax rates on financial transactions," reminding his readers that one good reason for low taxes on business deals is that the deals help raise capital, stimulating the nation's economy. But another reason for the low rates, Becker continued, is that "groups such as the New York

Stock Exchange lobby hard to keep taxes down." Lottery players, unlike stock traders, "are not well organized" and thus are powerless to persuade state lottery officials to be more generous about handing out prize money. The result is that while New Yorkers in slums and working class neighborhoods must pay a regressive 53 percent tax to place a bet, their fellow citizens from posh Park Avenue or the wealthy suburbs are paying a 33 percent capital gains tax on their business gambles. "In the long run," New Jersey state senator and lottery opponent John F. Russo said in 1989, a lottery "just alleviates the tax burden of the wealthiest."

Those who defend lotteries cannot deny that the games tax regressively, but they do argue that the levy may not be as regressive as it first appears. David Weinstein and Lillian Deitch, authors of a six-month study of lotteries and OTB conducted under a grant from the National Science Foundation, question whether it is even fair to consider regressivity in relation to legalized gambling. If a lottery allows a state to cut old regressive taxes on tobacco or liquor, or to avoid imposing new ones, then it is not so regressive after all. If it reduces or replaces a general sales tax, it's even less regressive. The use to which lottery revenues are put must also be considered, Weinstein and Deitch note. In Pennsylvania, proceeds go to help care for the elderly. Elderly Pennsylvanians who play the lottery—and lotteries are particularly popular among this age group—stand to benefit directly from their activity. The benefit makes the tax less regressive for senior citizens in the state. Anyway, says one state lottery director, even if lotteries do hit the poor harder than they hit the rich, so what? So does everything else. "Milk is regressive, bread is regressive," he told one reporter. "Anything the general public buys is regressive."

Nor, lottery defenders continue, is it true that lotteries appeal more to the needy than to the well-off. "There are no statistics out there that show the lottery preys on the impoverished," contends one lottery advertising agent. That may be the case. People who are truly impoverished may not have $1 to spare for a ticket. But lottery supporters contend that not even the working poor are disproportionately hurt by the games. They quote, for example, research done in 1974 and 1981 that seems to contradict the National Bureau of Economic Research finding. Those studies showed rich Americans spending about the same share of their income on lottery tickets as poorer ones. Another study, this one carried out at the University of Michigan, indicated that college graduates are twice as likely as high school dropouts to play the games. In 1987, the Opinion Research Corporation of Princeton, New Jersey, looked at Maine lottery players and reported that 60 percent claimed to have annual incomes between $20,000 and $70,000, while only 30 percent said they earned under $20,000 a year.

Lottery critics have little trouble faulting such arguments. A range of $20,000 to $70,000 is so wide. How many Mainers who play the lottery earn $21,000 or $22,000 a year compared with those who earn $68,000 or $69,000? they might ask. For the answer, they could consult the November 1988 issue of *Money* magazine. According to that source, a typical Maine ticket buyer makes $35,000 a year, enough for the state to rank, along with Delaware, as the one with the highest average income for lottery players. Players with the lowest average incomes—$20,460—live in the District of Columbia. Twenty thousand dollars was not a large amount to live on in the late 1980s, lottery critics assert, and since it was an average, many District players must earn considerably less. As far as the 1974 and 1981 studies are concerned, they go on, it's important to remember that they were conducted before lottomania hit the nation and turned millions of nongamblers into habitual ticket buyers. Were the studies' findings, cited in a 1989 column in *Fortune* magazine, still valid? The critics add that a California study indicated that the rich spend 0.3 percent of their income on lotteries; the poor, 2.1 percent. One, Charles Colson, wrote in the magazine *Christianity Today* of a Maryland survey that found the poorest one-third of state households buying one-half of the state's lottery tickets. Colson, incidentally, once acted as an aide to President Richard Nixon. Nixon, who became involved in a major political scandal, and was forced to resign from office in 1974. Colson spent time in prison for his part in the scandal. He later went into church work.

The critics further scorn the defense of lotteries on the grounds that they are no more regressive than a lot of other things. Just because one tax is regressive doesn't mean another ought to be. Just because poor Americans find it harder than rich ones to feed their families doesn't justify urging them to spend their food money on lottery tickets. Two wrongs don't make a right.

But those who favor lotteries have one more, and very powerful, point on their side: No one compels anyone to participate in the games. Urge them, yes. Tantalize them with visions of mega jackpots, yes. Downplay the overwhelming odds against winning, yes. Compel? No. The decision to buy a lottery ticket is up to each individual. Anyone who thinks lotteries are unfairly regressive, or too expensive, or just plain immoral, can simply walk away from them. That is the beauty of lotteries as a means of raising public revenues. With this kind of "tax," say Hoover Institution fellows Alvin Rabushka and Mikhail Bernstam, " 'Compliance' is 100%."

A Nation of Players—Who Wins?

A great many of them are complying, lottery officials are pleased to report. Thanks to heavy advertising and promotion, Americans are showing themselves increasingly willing to play the games. In Massachusetts and California, that willingness extends to 80 percent of the adult population. During 1988, New Yorkers spent an average of $91.17 on lottery tickets. In Pennsylvania, per person sales amounted to $121.48. On average, people in New Jersey laid out

$152.07, while those in Connecticut spent $158.53. Massachusetts, the national leader in per capita lottery sales, took in $234.92 for every Bay State resident. Totaled, that came to gross proceeds of $1.38 billion in 1988.

Not only are lottery proceeds in some states reaching into the billions, but those billions are also growing. In fiscal year 1987, New York took in gross revenues of $1.51 billion. Over the next twelve months, the figure rose $12 million to $1.63 billion. The state's 1988 net profit was $725.6 million. California's lottery grossed over $2.1 billion in 1988. Its net income: $804 million. Even in Montana, where a game did not begin until 1987, first-year proceeds were close to $22 million; net profit, $8.4 million.

How much is $8.4 million? Looked at one way, it is a lot. Eight and a half million dollars is almost exactly three times the $2.8 million the state of Hawaii spent on its police forces in 1986. It's a little more than Montana paid for employment security administration that same year.

Looked at another way, though, $8.4 million isn't so much. It's not even half again as much as Anhtinh Ton Giang won in the Ohio lottery in 1989. It's less than one-sixth of Sheelah Ryan's Florida win the year before and under one-thirteenth the size of Pennsylvania's mammoth $115 million 1989 jackpot. More to the point for Montanans, $8.4 million amounts to only a few percentage points of their state's annual budget.

That is typical. On average, the profit a state derives from its lottery comes to somewhere between one and 3 percent of state spending. Such percentages are not nearly enough, critics say, to justify the lotteries' downside—the regressivity of the tax they represent, the dent they make in the incomes of many working Americans, the deceptive advertising by which they are promoted. Some critics express particular concern about legalized gambling returns on the country's Native American reservations. Whereas the states pick up anywhere from 20 percent to 44 percent of gross lottery revenues, the tribes get from 12 percent to 18 percent, a ridiculously low share, many contend.

Expectably, lottery supporters—including those who sponsor the reservation games—do not share this negative perspective. Members of the Creek Nation of Oklahoma say they may wind up with only $3 million a year out of overall proceeds of $22 million, but that $3 million helps pay for educational, health, and social services, all of which might otherwise be lacking. The head of the Michigan lottery defends his operation by reminding people there that without 1987 ticket sales of a little over $1 billion, they would be forking over an average of $160 more a year in state taxes. That is a saving that cannot be ignored, one that benefits every Michigan taxpayer.

Who else benefits from the Michigan lottery—and from other legal and state and local gambling operations? Winners, of course, and the men and women employed by states and cities to direct the operations. Lottery advertising agents benefit as well. So do the banks responsible for handling lottery funds and tickets and the sales agents charged with selling the tickets. In one state alone, Maine, sales agents received $7 million in commissions for the fiscal year 1988.

Lotteries also produce indirect beneficiaries. Among them are the men and women who claim to have discovered the secret to winning the games. Some of these individuals have written so-called "dream books" that purport to tell people how to interpret their dreams to come up with their lucky numbers. Dreams have nothing to do with random drawings, but that fact doesn't stop these authors. Dream books have been sold in conjunction with other lotteries, including the infamous Louisiana lottery and past and present illegal numbers games.

Other indirect lottery winners may be corporations. One well-known and respected company presently cashing in on the lottery craze is Radio Shack, which offers for sale a random number generator described as "Your Own Personal Lottery Master, The Pocket

Computer That Picks The Numbers For You." Advertising for the gadget—1989 price, $24.95—ignores the fact that lottery computers can do the picking free of charge, just as well as and give players an equally good—or bad—chance of winning.

Other beneficiaries of lotteries include the entrepreneurs of LottoExpress, a company incorporated in Virginia that operates out of Jersey City, New Jersey. LottoExpress is in the business of buying lottery tickets and delivering them to out-of-state purchasers. Even telephone companies benefit from lottery activity, since they own the lines used to link computerized ticket machines with central terminals. But perhaps the best way to "win" at a lottery is to be in the business of supplying those computer systems and terminals to state lottery commissions.

Gtech Corporation of Providence, Rhode Island, is one lottery supplier. Founded in 1980 with $4.4 million, Gtech was reporting annual sales of $131 million seven years later. Not only do the people at Gtech and other supply companies provide lottery hardware, but they also design the contests, building in the odds requested by lottery commissions and taking care to make the games not only interesting but also adaptable so that the public can have the variety it craves. A supply company may also service the hardware it sells and rethink systems that don't work out as planned. When, for instance, New Jersey officials discovered that their instant game was bringing in only about 9 percent of lottery revenues while creating 90 percent of its paperwork, they called on their supplier to solve the problem. Now accounting is automatic in the New Jersey system. Other service company innovations: self-service ticket machines and radio links to outlying areas where telephones may not always operate at top efficiency.

Companies like Gtech, Control Data Corporation, and Scientific Games do not stop at selling lottery equipment. They also sell lotteries.

How so? Where lottery referendums have appeared on state

ballots, the companies have gone political, spending lavishly on advertising campaigns aimed at winning voter approval of the games. In many cases, the referendums have actually been written by men and women who work at those companies. Lottery supply people know that they are tapping into a profitable industry, and they are keen to see it expand. Already, by 1990, they had helped convince thirty-two states and the District of Columbia to hop on the lottery bandwagon. If wide-scale legalized gambling does invade the Southern Bible Belt—and many think it is only a matter of time before that happens—it will be thanks in part to staffers at places like Gtech and Scientific Games.

Lottery critics express dismay at the idea of permitting companies that stand to benefit from lotteries to draw up lottery referendums and promote gambling as a public policy. They are not happy to see dream book authors and corporations like Radio Shack profiting from the gullibility of some lottery players, either. The critics' voices, however, are hardly to be heard in the political debate. Others are louder: those of suppliers, ticket agents, bank officers, players, and, of course, the state officials whose departments share in lottery proceeds. It is, after all, those departments that gain most from the nation's official lotteries. Isn't it?

Winners Lose?

Bill Honig does not think so. Honig is the superintendent of public schools in California, one of eight states in which lottery profits are earmarked for education. In his view, California schools were better off in prelottery days. The reason: Taxpayers assume that schools get so much from the lottery that they don't need funds from other sources. "People think we're sitting on a pile of dough," Honig says, "when we're not." But the public perception that school districts are growing rich from the lottery makes it politically easy for state lawmakers to save money by cutting education spending. In fact, the California school department got 1.5 percent less of the overall state budget in 1988 than it had in 1986, a loss of $600 million a year.

Honig's experience also demonstrates the validity of a concern expressed by New Hampshire educators back in 1963. Those educators objected to funding public education by means of a lottery, warning that revenues would be variable, up in some years, down in others. True to their prediction, the California superintendent has watched with dismay while lottery income rises and sinks as new games and gimmicks are introduced and abandoned.

Honig isn't the only educator concerned about the effect lotteries may be having on public schools, and his state is not the only one where education funding decreased after becoming linked to a game. The Michigan, New Jersey, and Illinois school systems, also partially dependent upon lotteries, have suffered similarly. By 1989, the same fate was being forecast for Florida, where the lottery was bringing in just about enough to keep classrooms open for seven days out of the school year. "In many respects it is inappropriate to say that as the lottery goes up, education spending goes up," Robert H. Koff, dean of the School of Education at the State University of New York at Albany, was quoted as saying in 1989. New York is another state in which lottery proceeds help support the schools. "The public assumes there's a direct correlation between the amount of money the lottery brings in and the amount that goes to education. That's simply not the case." But another New York educator, Gregory Illenberg, pointed to a $3.6 billion increase in state aid to education between 1984 and 1989. "It's very unlikely that the governor and the legislature would have been that generous without the lottery," Illenberg concluded. And so the debate over the merits of state-sponsored lotteries goes on.

It's a debate that extends beyond the monetary to the social. What effect, some people wonder, do the games have on individuals? On society as a whole?

Researchers David Weinstein and Lillian Deitch, writing in the early 1970s, downplayed the social consequences of legalized gambling. Lotteries, they concluded, were not likely to have adverse effects upon "the personal, familial or work situations of the average bettor or family." The reason for that, the two believed, is that a lottery is not the sort of game that attracts or produces players who bet so heavily that they get in over their heads, losing their savings and self-respect—perhaps even their jobs and families. Lotteries, they and others argue, are not sufficiently involving to appeal to gambling addicts or potential addicts. Casinos, racetracks, poker parlors, and the like—these are what attract certain kinds of addictive personalities and help to produce compulsive gamblers. Strolling up to a lottery terminal in the neighborhood supermarket and casually buying a ticket simply cannot be compared to putting money on the favorite at a noisy, crowded racetrack, breathlessly watching as a roulette wheel spins to a stop, or adding to the pot on the strength of what looks like a winning hand. Lotteries represent a different type of gamble altogether, their defenders maintain.

The argument leaves lottery critics cold. If lottery officials haven't made their games as exciting and involving as other gambling activities, they protest, it is not for want of trying. Why are new games constantly being introduced—along with new twists, new colors, new promises—if not to get people involved? Obviously involvement is the aim. Why else the ads that solicit daydreams about the spending of prize money? Why else the "directions" about the preferred way to choose a number or scratch an instant ticket? Why else the promotions some have labeled fraudulent? Lotteries may have been noninvolving when Weinstein and Deitch did their research and wrote their book over fifteen years ago, the critics acknowledge. But they aren't necessarily that way anymore.

A Nation of Gamblers

Evidence that the critics may be right comes from the trade journal

Gambling & Wagering Business. According to the magazines's figures, the gross amount bet in legal games in 1987 was $210.8 billion, up from $125.7 billion in 1982. Factor in the amount spent on illegal bets, and the figures are $151.2 billion in 1982; $252.8 billion in 1987. The 1987 sum totals to approximately $1,000 for every man, woman, and child in the country. It represents a gambling increase of 67 percent over just five years, a substantial hike. Not nearly as substantial, though, as the hike in state lottery betting over the same five-year period—317 percent.

What does it mean that the amount of money bet in state lotteries more than tripled between 1982 and 1987? For one thing, the critics say, not only are Americans gambling, but many of them—like the one who claimed to be betting the mortgage money on Pennsylvania's $115 million game—are gambling with funds they can ill afford to lose. The mortgage claim may have been an exaggeration, but it is a fact that people are more willing that ever before to spend on lotteries. According to financial writer Sylvia Porter, single-person purchases of up to $5,000 dollars' worth of tickets for just one jackpot have been documented.

The enormous increase in lottery betting further indicates that the states have succeeded in making gambling attractive to hundreds of thousands of people who would otherwise never have engaged in such activity. They have made it attractive even to people who may previously have disapproved of it. Iowa took just eight years to evolve from a place where popular attitudes made church bingo illegal to one in which adults can bet in two different lotteries, at cardrooms and racetracks, on riverboats and via television. What is more, the states have managed to make gambling seem harmless, even public-spirited. Just a few years ago, most Americans thought of gambling as something that might be fun but that had its disreputable side. Most associated it with corruption and crime. No more. "What state lotteries have done," says Valerie Lorenz of the National Center for

Pathological Gambling, "is to take the specter of immorality away and elevate gambling into an act of civic responsibility."

Bill Eadington, economics professor at the University of Nevada at Reno, agrees that the games have had that effect. "The lotteries were the catalyst, the driving force, in changing public attitudes toward gambling," he believes. "They exposed people to gambling who knew little about it." Those who support the games admit that the exposure is taking place, but they contend that the vast majority of lottery players will limit their involvement to the purchase of a couple of tickets weekly. Few if any will become addicted to gambling.

Perhaps so, perhaps not. One New Jersey woman stole $38,000 to support her devotion to the state lottery. A young Pennsylvania man lost $6,000 trying to win a $2.5 million jackpot. In despair, he attempted suicide.

Some who belong to Gamblers Anonymous (G.A.), an organization devoted to helping compulsive bettors kick their habit, trace the origins of that habit to state games. One member, a man identified in G.A. style simply as Jack T., says he became addicted to the Maryland lottery. After spending up to $400 a week and exhausting his bank account, he embezzled $14,000—and kept on playing. "The fear of getting caught didn't stop me . . . " he says now. "The fear of jail, the fear of losing my wife—nothing stopped me from gambling."

Jack T. may blame the lottery for his addiction, but others in G.A. concede that gamblers are more often born than made. "Most experts agree that legalization creates few compulsive gamblers," a spokesperson for the group says. "Anyone interested in placing a bet will find a way to do it." However, the problem as G.A. and other lottery critics see it is that the state games are piquing that interest and, as a result, setting people who never thought of gambling on the road to addiction. The National Commission on Gambling, for instance, predicts an increase in female addicts as a result of lotteries. Richard Richardson of the Maryland Council on Compulsive Gambling makes the same prediction. Women, aware of the stigma long attached to gambling, are more likely to play the lottery than to go to a casino or out to the track, he believes. "It's less time-consuming and it's not conspicuous."

Richardson believes teenagers and children may become addicted as well. "Where it might be difficult for a 15-year-old to get into a race track or drive to Atlantic City, he can walk into a 7-Eleven and spend $10 to buy lottery tickets," he explains. Although it is against the law to sell tickets to minors, such sales have occurred. The growing popularity of self-service lottery terminals could make teen buying even more common. Machines can't detect a person's age. New Jersey's John Russo also worries about the surge in gambling among the nation's elderly. "Those senior citizens standing on the line at the drugstore in Ocean County would never play an illegal numbers racket with a bookie," he points out. "They wouldn't know where to find one." They know where to find lottery terminals and buses to Atlantic City casinos, though.

Will finding them lead to their searching out an illegal bookie operation? Lottery supporters may say not, but some of the facts suggest otherwise. As we saw in Chapter 2, legal games have in the past given rise to illegal ones. They're doing the same today. Just as big-city numbers games developed out of the authorized lotteries of the nineteenth century, so the illegal operators of the 1990s may use winning state numbers to determine their own winners. Since such operators return a significantly greater percentage of proceeds to bettors than state lottery commissions do, the incentive for people to switch from legal to illegal activity is strong. Some who do make the switch may end up in serious trouble. Gambling, according to Richard Richardson, can be "a perfectly healthy form of recreation for 96 percent of the population." For the other 4 percent, it something more menacing.

What Kind of Message?

Should the states be in the business of tempting that 4 percent? That's what lottery critics want to know, and they have other questions as well. Should governments be promoting gambling in order to pay a negligible portion of their bills? Should they set up lottery commissions and encourage them to tax regressively, operate expensively, and advertise unscrupulously? Should vital services like public education and transportation be dependent, even in part, upon the whims of lottery players? Should Americans be encouraged to believe that luck alone solves problems? "All of us feel a little queasy as a school system based on gambling," California's Bill Honig asserts. "What kind of message is that to kids: That you don't have to work hard because lightning will come from the blue?"

It's a lousy message—on that, lottery critics are agreed. But the critics are very much in the minority, and their voices are, John Russo ruefully admits, weak. Millions upon millions of Americans regard state-sponsored games and other forms of legalized gambling as fun and a great solution to pressing financial problems. Some, like researchers Weinstein and Deitch, see gambling as a solution to other problems as well. To them, being able to place a bet—legally or illegally—gives the needy a sense of hope for a better future. "From this point of view," they contend, "provision of a legal outlet can be construed as fulfilling a social need."

That's a contention guaranteed to outrage lottery critics. Not that the critics deny that the need is there. It definitely is. As Americans entered the final decade of the twentieth century, figures from the U.S. Bureau of the Census showed that about one in every seven was living in poverty. During a thirty-two-month period between 1983 and 1986, the last years for which such statistics are available, 18.3 percent of the U.S. population received aid from a major state or federal welfare program. Indications were that the percentage increased substantially in 1990. Estimates of the number of homeless people nationwide ranged up to three million.

But is legalized gambling the best hope we have to offer these people? What about training and education programs to enable them to get better jobs? What about an even higher minimum wage? More affordable housing? Middle-class Americans often gripe about seeing the poor spending money—sometimes money taken from welfare checks—on lottery tickets. It's true enough that the sight can be infuriating. Are these bettors depriving their children of food? people wonder. Letting a gambling habit keep them from being good parents? But if we defend lotteries on the grounds that they fill a void in the lives of the poor, how can we turn around and blame the poor for taking advantage of what we're offering them?

And isn't it presumptuous—or downright paternalistic—for richer people to be telling poorer ones how best to run their lives? "We think it's OK for everybody, including poor people, to choose our elected officials," J. Blaine Lewis, director of the Connecticut State lottery said in a December 1988 interview in *USA Today*. "But then somehow, when it comes to spending a dollar on a lottery ticket, we're not sure they're competent to make that decision. That's a double standard." Lewis has a point—but so do those who worry about the kind of effect regressive lottery "taxes" may be having on needy American families.

Other social problems seem to require more creative solutions than the faint promise held forth by a lottery. A good portion of the country's elderly live alone, cut off by distance, by disagreement, or by divorce from brothers and sisters, children, grandchildren, and old friends. Many are lonely, and their loneliness, psychologists say, is a large part of what drives such a high percentage of them to gamble. So why not tackle the loneliness issue head-on? Couldn't we have more centers where the elderly can congregate and socialize? Places where young and old can come into contact? Programs to enable senior citizens to share their knowledge, skills, and experience with people of all ages?

What about problems on Native American reservations, problems like poor nutrition among children, low levels of education, rampant alcoholism? These are genuine problems. Do we really think they are going to be solved by gaming operations that produce net proceeds of a few million dollars a year?

What about the problem of decaying urban areas like Atlantic City? Casino gambling was supposed to bring new life to the place, to produce jobs and stimulate a building boom. It didn't. The first Atlantic City casino opened in 1978, and eleven years later, *Time* magazine noted, the town had 18,103 slot machines—and not a single car wash or movie theater. It had one supermarket and had lost 20 percent of its people. Of those who remained, 75 percent officially ranked as poor. So much for casinos as Atlantic City problem solvers.

So much, lottery critics would say, for any type of gaming operation as a solution to social ills. Gambling is no substitute for hard work.

It never has been. Captain John Smith called the Virginia Company's Jamestown lottery the "real and substantiall food" that enabled the colony to survive. But was it? American historian Samuel Eliot Morison didn't so much as mention the lottery in writing about Jamestown's transformation from destitute and demoralized settlement to thriving town. The colony's early troubles, Morison wrote, stemmed in good measures from the fact that its first settlers "seem to have been divided into those who could not and those who would not work." Once the colonists gave up the idea that they were going to strike it rich by happening across New World gold and buckled down to raising tobacco and selling it, their fortunes began looking up. Getting the opportunity to own property and gaining a measure of self-rule helped, too. So did the arrival of women—and later, of children. However John Smith may have seen things, it was hard work and a sense of responsibility, not a lottery, that enabled Jamestowners to solve their problems.

Those who stand against state lotteries and other legalized gambling operations say that it is hard work and the taking of responsibility that will enable us to solve our problems. In the critics' view, much of the work and responsibility needs to come from the nation's leaders. It's about time for our elected and appointed officials to stop seeking reelection with no-new-taxes promises—and to stop trying to paper over economic reality with a glittering facade of lotteries and other government-sponsored gambling activities. It's about time, too, for them to begin telling Americans the blunt truth: that if they want good schools, adequate health care, safe public transportation, and all the rest, they must pay for them.

Conservative columnist George F. Will expressed this idea eloquently in a 1989 issue of *Newsweek* magazine. "Once upon a time," he wrote, "social health was thought to be connected with the political courage to ask, and the civic virtue to grant, taxes sufficient to pay the price of . . . necessary public services." Charles Colson said the same thing more simply: "If revenues are necessary, legislators should raise taxes."

Of course, legislators are not the only ones with a duty to reassume the responsibility for making tough decisions about taxes and other public policy matters. All Americans, people like Colson and Will believe, need to follow the example set by seventeenth century Jamestowners. We need to abandon notions about money growing on trees and pots of gold waiting to be picked up at the ends of rainbows. We need to recognize that what we want to have, we ourselves must be responsible for providing.

As a first step, Americans might take a closer look at what that provision really costs. The $1,194.5 trillion 1988 tax bill averaged out to payments of just $4,944 per person. Canadians paid about the same in 1988, $4,820 apiece. People who paid more included Austrians

($5,281 each); Belgians ($5,302); Netherlanders ($5,483); West Germans ($5,484); Finns ($5,499); the French ($5,802); and the Swiss ($6,707). The highest individual tax bills came in Sweden and Norway, where, in 1988, people paid $8,385 and $8,346 each, respectively. The U.S. tax system is designed in a way that hits the middle class especially hard, but as a group, we Americans are not as overtaxed as many of us believe. Perhaps that tax structure needs rethinking. And perhaps state lotteries— and other tax-substituting forms of legalized gambling—are not as vital to the U.S. national interest as we and our leaders have managed to convince ourselves they are.

6

"This Age of Lotteries"

"Megalotteries present the most painless imaginable way to collect revenues desperately needed for good works . . . " novelist and screenwriter Jesse Hill Ford wrote in a May 1989 column in *USA Today.* "There should be a reduce-the-deficit lottery . . . ; then one for defense, another for health and human services, and so on right down to landscaping for the White House lawn and congressional salaries."

A few months later, in September, columnist and commentator Andy Rooney came up with an even more drastic-sounding suggestion. "Maybe we ought to . . . raise all government money by betting on everything," he wrote. Even election outcomes could be determined by means of fund-raising lotteries. "Every four years, we'd all be able to bet on our choice for the presidency. The candidate wouldn't be elected by the number of votes. The candidate who had the most money bet on him or her would be the winner." And of course the victor would enter the White House with a full treasury.

Rooney was writing tongue in cheek, of course, and so, probably, was Ford. But Hoover Institution researchers Alvin Rabushka and Mikhail Bernstam were quite serious when, a few months earlier, in February 1989, they had used the pages of *Fortune* magazine to call for establishing a national lottery. The two proposed designating the game's proceeds for worthwhile purposes, "thereby giving participants a humanitarian motivation." Those purposes: " . . . the very programs for which Congress is likely to appropriate new funds . . . help for the homeless, for instance, and cleaning up the environment."

Paul Magnusson, halfheartedly endorsing a federal lottery two months later in the publication *Business Week,* echoed both the humanitarian theme and the environmental one. "In appealing to altruism, a national lottery could shine, too," he argued. "Worried about the environment? Play the Environmental Protection Agency's Green Lottery."

A National Lottery—A Good Idea?

In analyzing the pros and cons of instituting a national lottery, Magnusson recapitulated the ancient arguments in favor of such a game: It would be fun and would be a tax people would be eager to pay. It wouldn't even really be an encouragement to vice, he claimed, since in the eyes of many economists, an official lottery does not represent gambling so much as it does "an excise tax on a commodity—a lottery ticket that happens to be supplied by a government monopoly that sets the price." It's the only kind of new tax, Magnusson intimated, that members of both political parties, Democratic and Republican, as well as President Bush, might be glad to ask the nation to pay. Finally, if federal tax forms were designed to include a space for taxpayers to write in the amount they wanted to bet each year, they might attract a surprisingly large number of players. Charles Clotfelter, an economist at Duke University in North Carolina, believes making such a space available would encourage wagering by "people who might be embarrassed to step up and make a bet publicly."

Yet Magnusson saw difficulties in the way of imposing even this kind of backdoor tax. State governments would likely oppose a national lottery, for instance, on the assumption that it would cut into the proceeds of their own games. And he conceded that lotteries are regressive, implying that there might well be opposition on that score. Besides, "moralists" might "howl" about gambling's effect upon the poor. On balance, though, a national lottery struck Magnusson as a good idea. Or at least as an inevitable one, what with regional contests like Tri-State Megabucks and Lotto America already operating on an interstate basis. "Let the games begin," he concluded.

Rabushka and Bernstam showed themselves more solidly in favor of a federal lottery. They were specially optimistic about the amount of money it would generate. "It would be a mistake to underestimate the revenue-raising potential of a national lottery," they wrote. "The program could award prizes significantly bigger even than the recent $61.9 million jackpot in California." Their projection for annual proceeds: over $18 billion a year; half of it to be spent on prizes and expenses, half to go to the U.S. Treasury as profit. That profit would come at little social cost, the Hoover researchers thought. Unlike Magnusson, they had little concern about a lottery's regressivity and quoted studies—one of them a decade and a half old—indicating that well-off Americans buy tickets as often as poor ones. In any case, federal lottery ticket buyers would not necessarily be U.S. citizens, as "Lottery revenues would be increased by permitting foreigners to purchase tickets." Another advantage of a legal national game as Rabushka and Bernstam saw it, "Legal lotteries divert cash from illegal gambling, like the numbers racket, weakening organized crime."

Not everyone—not even all lottery supporters—accept the contention that legal gambling cuts down on the illegal variety. Nor do they necessarily share an enthusiasm for a national lottery. J. Blaine Lewis, whom we met in Chapter 5, was not only director of the Connecticut State lottery in 1989, but also president of the North American Association of State and Provincial Lotteries. His jobs made him a backer of state lotteries—but not of a federal one. In his *USA Today* interview, he pointed to the roadblocks the states might try to put in the way of a national game. And he downplayed the contribution such a game would make to the federal money situation. A yearly profit of $6 billion was more likely than one of $9 billion, he thought, and what was $6 billion compared to a national debt of $3 *trillion?*

Others concur in Lewis's reservations—and give voice to further reservations of their own. The regressivity of lotteries; the fact that most studies show that they do hit harder at working class budgets than at middle- and upper-class ones; their historical links to increases in illegal gambling; and the disappointment they have proved to supposed beneficiaries like the California public schools—each is mentioned in turn. So is the distaste many Americans feel at seeing governments, above all the federal government, in the business of promoting gambling. The idea that the United States would try to attract gamblers from other countries adds another level of discomfort for some people. Why would Mexicans and Canadians—our closest neighbors and most likely lottery customers—bother to contribute to an American game anyway? They have contests of their own that they might consider more "patriotic" to play.

Other Lotteries / Other Gambles

Whether or not the United States does adopt a national lottery, it's a safe bet that gambling will continue to become a more and more common American pastime, for a while at least. As of 1990, voters in only one state, North Dakota, had ever turned down a lottery referendum question. As was mentioned in Chapter 5, most experts expect lottery pressure in the Southern Bible Belt to overwhelm the area and lead to changes in policy there.

More business promotion lotteries and sweepstakes are likely in the coming months and years as well. Even state and national lobbying organizations are getting into the act. Early in 1990, the American

Association of Retired People (AARP), which promotes public policies aimed at benefiting men and women aged fifty or more, sent ballots to members to enable them to vote for delegates to the group's soon-to-be-held Florida convention. "By casting your ballot," the accompanying literature read, "you'll **automatically** be entered in our *Special 1990 Convention Sweepstakes*." Top prizes would be ten free trips (five days/four nights) to the meeting; 500 runners-up were to get "specially designed AARP Tote Bags," and 100 more, free copies of a written guide to financial planning. In Maine, an antinuclear activist group holds a yearly fund-raising raffle. Participants in its 1990 contest could purchase any number of $1 tickets on a chance to win a seven-day Caribbean vacation for two. Solicitations mailed to thousands of Maine homes included twelve tickets and checkoff spaces for entrants:

( ) I am enclosing the stubs of _____ tickets and $_____.

( ) Please rush me _____ more tickets!

And, acknowledging that those with antinuclear sentiments may also be antilottery:

( ) I hate raffles. Here's a donation of $_____.

Another new lottery possibility exists within the U.S. Army. In 1988, the Armed Services Committee of the U.S. House of Representatives asked Department of Defense (DOD) officials to conduct a survey to determine the merits of allowing servicemen and women based outside the country to bet in an official lottery. The committee was acting in response to a DOD budget crunch that threatened to cut back on family and recreation programs for members of the military. According to John Hughes of *The Christian Science Monitor*, Army officials were "extraordinarily coy" about answering his questions relevant to the study.

Their coyness did not surprise Hughes. "Is the Army less than enthusiastic about publicizing a potentially embarrassing project?" he asked. It ought to be, he thought. Of the more than half a million Americans then stationed on overseas military posts, Hughes estimated that 20 percent were under age twenty-one and another 35 percent between the ages of twenty-two and twenty-five. Should the U.S. government be introducing these young, perhaps lonely and vulnerable men and women to the thrill of betting "at a time when questions are being increasingly raised about the addiction of Americans to gambling?" Hughes may not have thought so, but a majority of the House Armed Services Committee seems to have regarded the idea more favorably.

Still another area ripe for gambling growth, the experts say: casinos. Nevada and Atlantic City led the way, and the action is spreading. As we saw, casino gambling began in 1989 in Deadwood, South Dakota, and overnight, gaming rooms sprang up throughout the town, in taverns and drugstores, in supermarkets and motels, and at gas stations. When Iowans approved riverboat gambling to be based in the town of Davenport, it was by a 60–40 margin. Voters there were clearly impressed by a study suggesting that a yearly seven-month riverboat season would stimulate $69 million in new spending, create 2,350 new jobs, and produce $490,000 in new local tax revenues, as well as $1.2 million for the state. Increased tourist traffic might necessitate a new hotel and restaurant.

As the 1990s began, men and women in other parts of the Midwest were looking enviously at Davenport's prospects. In the economically depressed steel town of Gary, Indiana, voters approved a casino referendum by the same 60–40 margin that had carried the day in Iowa and began pressing state legislators to allow them to begin operations. Many in Detroit, Michigan, once—but no more—the automobile-manufacturing capital of the world, also favor a state go-ahead for casino operations.

Will casino gambling, if approved, solve the problems of cities like Detroit and Gary, though? It didn't solve Atlantic City's. In Atlantic City, the first decade of casino gambling was accompanied by a 20 percent population loss. Seventy-five percent of the people still living there are mired in poverty. Casinos haven't brought those people supermarkets or car washes or movie theaters. "It's anybody's guess" whether casino gambling will do any better by Deadwood after its novelty wears off, one local hotel owner says. In Davenport, the concern centers on what some call "gambling overload." By 1989, two full years before the riverboats were set to begin operations, Iowans were already showing symptoms of tiring of some of the gambling options available to them. A Des Moines racetrack was experiencing serious losses, for example. Has Iowa gone too far?

Perhaps, but even if it has, it seems unlikely that its example will put much of a crimp in gambling activities nationwide. In fact, a whole new type of legalized gambling is, people like Connecticut lottery director Lewis believe, about to be introduced around the country. "The next thing on the horizon," Lewis told *USA Today*, "will be sports betting . . . . It would probably start out with so-called cards. On one package, there would be maybe six games, and you would try to guess the winner of as many games as you could."

Sports Betting

It didn't take long for Lewis's prediction to begin coming true. On September 6, 1989, Oregon became the first—and so far only—state to take on the role of bookmaker for professional football. (Although sports betting has long been legal in Nevada, it operates there through privately owned casinos. A 1976 football betting scheme in Delaware expired after one season.)

Proceeds from the Oregon scheme, which is run by the state's lottery commission, were to help pay for sports programs at the state's public colleges and universities. The betting involved, as Lewis had predicted, wagering on the outcomes of anywhere from four to fourteen National Football League (NFL) games. Bets were to range in size from $1 to $20, and no limit was set on the number of bets that might be placed. To win, a bettor had to guess right on every game. In its first year, the Oregon operation did not include the placing of bets on individual teams. That may come, though. "Later on," J. Blaine Lewis also said in 1988, "you could even have head-to-head betting . . . as the illegal people do now."

State sponsorship of professional sports betting is controversial, even in this gambling-happy day and age. Lottery officials, aware of the difficulties involved in getting more and more players to part with more and more cash month after month, may like the idea. But the notion of betting on something they regard as a purely sporting event bothers a lot of people on pro organizations. For one thing, sports gambling introduces a business element to what is supposed to be a contest of strength and skill. "These are not horses," Charles Grantham, executive director of the National Basketball Association's (NBA) Players' Association, told Oregon lottery officials when, in November 1989, they considered incorporating pro basketball into state gambling activities. "We're dealing with people. We just don't think they should be bet on." James Heffernan, NFL public relations director, expressed another concern. "It's the perception that teams and players are involved that we object to," Heffernan explained.

Of course, player involvement could be more than a mere perception. That's another worry. What if team members bet on a game's outcome, then threw a game in order to beat the odds and make a bundle? Such corruption has occurred. Rent the 1988 movie *Eight Men Out* and watch how some of the Chicago White Sox—who have gone down in history as the Chicago Black Sox—conspired to lose the 1919 World Series. Or a team's manager, or some of its members, could direct or play just carelessly enough to shave a few points off the final score. Since the projected point spread is calculated into betting odds, point shaving could be a profitable exercise for the unscrupulous.

Worries about shaved points and thrown games are natural since sports gambling, for the most part illegal in this country, has traditionally been associated with organized crime. "We don't feel team sports should be connected with gambling in any way, shape, or form," James Heffernan said shortly before Oregon went ahead and made its connection. But others defend state sponsorship of NFL and NBA gambling precisely because they believe the result will be to reduce illegal activity. One Oregon football fan told *The New York Times* that he planned to stop patronizing illegal bookies and start playing the state's game. "All this does is give a legal outlet to what millions of people do every week in their homes and offices," he said.

Richard Mosiman, a vice squad police detective in Portland, Oregon, isn't so sure about that. "This game could have the effect of introducing a whole new group of people to illegal gambling," he worries. "The state's game is a sucker's game." That's because lottery officials return such a low percentage—typically 50 percent or less—in prizes. "Once the gambler becomes somewhat knowledgeable," Sergeant Mosiman continues, "he'll realize there's a better game down the street with the illegal bookmaker."

Even if he doesn't, others say, there's a chance the lottery's football game will turn him—or her—into an addicted gambler. There is no way a state lottery official can argue that sports betting is nonaddictive. "I shudder when I think of the implications of this game," Valerie Lorenz of the National Center for Pathological Gambling, Incorporated, said the day Oregon inaugurated its football scheme. Nor would it be easy for supporters of state-sponsored sports betting to maintain that indulging in such activity would have little or no effect on the budgets of the poor. A bet of $20 is no small matter, especially when there is no limit on the number of bets that can be made.

Concerns like those expressed relative to the Oregon game may help keep officially sponsored pro sports gambling from catching on in other states. Massachusetts officials expressed interest in the idea, and so did lottery commissioners in Connecticut and New Hampshire. In Kentucky, plans to have the state take bets on football games were actually drawn up. In that state, famous for its horse racing, track owners concerned about such betting affecting their profits got the state to drop its plans. Pressure from NFL officials put Delaware's football game out of business after its first year. But even if sports betting fails to spread in the 1990s as state lotteries did in the 1980s, state gambling operations, particularly lottery-type contests, seem set to stay around for a while at least. Is there, the critics ask, any way to reform those operations in order to limit what some see as their more harmful respects?

Gambling Reform

One possible reform would be to impose a money ceiling on jackpots. The thought of a single individual walking away with a $55 million prize strikes a lot of people as ridiculous. Who needs that much? "Only the greediest players or prospective players complained that the jackpots of Lotto 48, never less than $3 million, were not big enough," Zachary Berman wrote to *The New York Times* when state officials transformed Lotto 48 into Lotto 54. The transformation came in the name of creating larger jackpots—thereby attracting more players. But Berman himself would be quite happy with $3 million, and so would most of the rest of us. In fact, the Brooklyn man went on, "The latest change is likely to drive away players like myself." Lottery commissioners can't seem to shake their belief that only ever larger prizes will keep the dollars flowing. But can jackpots rise forever? Won't a great many people eventually come around to Berman's point of view and stop buying tickets? If that happens, the lottery bubble will surely burst. Wouldn't it be in a state's own best interests to keep jackpots within reasonable limits—and keep players involved?

Another reform idea is to require the states, and the federal government, too, should it adopt a public or semipublic lottery, to abide by the same truth-in-advertising rules they expect the officers of private enterprises to observe. Such a reform could have a dramatic impact on lottery commercials. The odds against winning might have to be clearly stated in print and broadcast ads, for example, no longer confined to the small print on the back of a ticket. "Everybody wins" implications might be dropped. Sales pitches could be made more upfront about the amounts winners can really expect to get and the way in which they can expect to get them. They could also be more specific about the difference between winning $30 or $40 million and being handed a free new ticket. And the Federal Trade Commission, or some other government agency, might be given powers of enforcement over advertising for legalized gambling activities.

Another truth-in-advertising reform could be to require state promotions to include information about the possibility that the kind of behavior they urge can lead to the illness we call addictive gambling. Some other advertisers must already adhere to such requirements. By law, tobacco product ads and packages must carry a clear warning about smoking's addictive qualities and its proven harmful effects on human health. Many over-the-counter drugs come with directions about use—or nonuse—for children. Shouldn't ads for legalized gambling be equally forthright?

State gambling officials and the advertising agencies they hire might argue that they already are. A 1989 subway ad for New York's OTB operation, for instance, included a cautionary note: "Bet with your head . . . not over it." Critics, though, were not satisfied by the "warning." A clever pun, it might be, but few would call it a very direct message to the 4 percent of Americans in danger of falling prey to a compulsive gambling habit. Anyway, as *The New York Times* said in an editorial, the warning's type was "so tiny that only the most searching straphanger can read it." The ad in question was the "Everybody Loves [for which read 'Is'] a Winner" one. Plainly visible below that headline, *The Times* noted, inch-high letters proclaimed, "That's Why We All Belong at OTB." Not all of us, as Gamblers Anonymous members like Jack T. would attest.

Are truth-in-advertising rules likely to be applied to state gambling operations? Other reforms imposed? Not if state lottery officials and others involved in legalized gambling have their way. As they see matters, putting such reforms in place would mean the beginning of the end for their businesses. Warn gamblers that they risk becoming addicted? Millions of Americans threw away their cigarettes after reading and hearing tobacco warnings. What will happen to tax-substituting lotteries and other gambling schemes if people listen to warnings about them? What if lottery ads are forced to be honest about the likelihood of winning a megabucks game? Who would purchase a ticket on a chance to win $115 million understanding that the odds of taking home the prize were roughly the same as the odds of living to the age of 116? Not very many people. Certainly not enough to pull even a few million dollars a year into a state treasury.

Putting a lid on lottery prizes is another bad idea, most lottery officials further agree. After all the hoopla about $115 million jackpots and $55 million wins, who's going to bother to gamble for "only" a couple of million? No one—or so lottery officials believe. In their view, the states cannot afford to cut back on their gambling operations in any way. They cannot afford to stop their headlong rush toward bigger and bigger jackpots, toward more and more advertising and promotion, toward new games, new excitement, new players. They cannot afford to follow any other course than that of doing more today of what they did yesterday—and of doing still more of the same tomorrow.

That's how it is with an addiction. What was once a matter of choice becomes a necessity, then a compulsion. And the addiction can be as real for a public entity as for a private individual. The states, cities, and other groups that sponsor America's legalized gambling activities are, lottery critics charge, risking becoming as addicted to their habit as any Gamblers Anonymous member could ever be. Unless checked, the public addition, like an individual's, may feed upon itself, growing monstrously. And last, people like George Will and others fear that addiction could devour much of what has made our American democracy great.

"Once upon a time," writes the conservative Will, "mass irrationality was considered a menace to democratic government. In this age of lotteries, manufacturing mobs is a government goal and mass hysteria is an important ingredient of public finance." From a different spot on the political spectrum, Democrat John Russo agrees. Thanks to lotteries, the New Jersey state lawmaker says, "This is becoming a sick, sick, sick society."

A New End to Lotteries?

Can it cure itself? It must, those who agree with Russo and Will believe, or a cure will be forced upon it. We are experiencing, says I. Nelson Rose, professor at Whittier College in California and a specialist in the law as it applies to gambling, the third great gambling wave in U.S. history. The first wave began in colonial times and ended with the reform movement of the first half of the nineteenth century. The second started with the end of the Civil War and culminated in the downfall of the Louisiana lottery. The third boom in gambling, Rose wrote in 1989, will encompass the 1990s and the first decade of the twenty-first century. "The end will come," he predicts, "when the general population says, 'This is too much.' "

How does Rose envision the end being triggered? By scandals, which he sees as "inevitable given the cash involved." He points out that state lotteries, for example, the one in Pennsylvania, have already

101

been rigged by insiders. But other circumstances, Rose contends, will also contribute to curtailing the boom.

"Sports betting will speed the fall," he wrote. "Think of the message that the state as bookie is giving our children: 'It's not whether you win or lose but if you beat the spread.' Other factors include gambling by children, suicides and embezzlements; simply too much hard sell. Add in a national desire to return to traditional values, and everything we see about us will once again be outlawed."

America's few lottery critics may hope Rose will turn out to be right. But its millions of lottery players would probably label his predictions as preposterous. And they'd be willing to bet against them ever coming true.

Notes By Chapter

Chapter 1

Adler, Bill, Jr. *The Lottery Book*. New York: Bill Adler Books, Inc., William Morrow and Company, 1986.

McKinney, Rhoda E. "Has Money Spoiled the Lottery Millionaires?" *Ebony*, December 1988.

Magnusson, Paul. "A National Lottery Is Not Such a Long Shot." *Business Week*, April 10, 1989.

Marrino, Vivian. "Lottery Winners Adrift in Sea of High Finance." *Morris County Daily Record*, February 12, 1989.

Rabushka, Alvin, and Mikhail S. Bernstam. "To Keep the Tax Promise, Try a Lottery." *Fortune*, February 27, 1989.

Chapter 2

Findlay, John M. *People of Chance: Gambling in American Society from Jamestown to Las Vegas*. New York: Oxford University Press, 1986.

Jackson, Shirley. *The Lottery and Other Stories*. New York: Farrar, Straus, Giroux, 1949, 1982.

"Lottery picks . . . " *USA Today*, August 3, 1989.

Morison, Samuel Eliot. *The Oxford History of the American People*. New York: Oxford University Press, 1965.

Peterson, Virgil W. *Gambling, Should It Be Legalized?* Springfield, Ill.: Charles C. Thomas, 1951.

Weinstein, David, and Lillian Deitch. *The Impact of Legalized Gambling: The Socioeconomic Consequences of Lotteries and Off-Track Betting*. New York: Praeger Publishers, 1974.

Chapter 3

Atchison, Sandra D. "Bingo! Are Indian Tribes Hitting the Jackpot?" *Business Week*, April 24, 1989.

Church, George J. "Why Pick on Pete?" *Time*, July 10, 1989.

Cook, James. "Lottomania." *Forbes*, March 6, 1989.

Egan, Timothy. "Oregon Inaugurates Football Betting." *The New York Times*, September 7, 1989.

Farmer, John J. "The Land of Odds." *The Star-Ledger*, September 17, 1989.

Findlay, John M. *People of Chance.*

Johnson, Dirk. "Gambling Returns to Town of Legend." *The New York Times*, November 2, 1989.

"Quack! Quack! Quack!" *Time*, December 4, 1989.

Thomas, William V. *Gambling's New Respectability*. Washington, D.C.: Congressional Quarterly, 1979.

Weinstein, David, and Lillian Deitch, *The Impact of Legalized Gambling: The Socioeconomic Consequences of Lotteries and Offtrack Betting.*

Welles, Chris. "America's Gambling Fever." *Business Week*, April 24, 1989.

Chapter 4

Adler, Bill, Jr. *The Lottery Book.*

Berman, Zachary M. "New York State's Lottery Has Reached the Point of Lunacy." *The New York Times*, September 18, 1988 (letter to editor).

Colson, Charles. "The Myth of the Money Tree." *Christianity Today*, July 10, 1987.

Cook, James. "Lottomania."

Jones, Alex S. " '$35 M and She's Single!' Turns Into 'Reporters Bite Again!' " *The New York Times*, January 9, 1990.

Kreis, Donald M. "The Lottery Frenzy." *Maine Times*, July 14, 1989.

Lemaire, Jean. "After 553,058 Years, a Win!" *The New York Times*, May 6, 1989.

"Lottery Rot." *The Christian Science Monitor*, January 22, 1990.

Navarro, Mireya. "Big Jackpot, Big Dollars, Big Dreams." *The New York Times*, January 6, 1990.

"Odds and Ends." *The Wall Street Journal*, May 15, 1989.

Porter, Sylvia. "Lottery Fever—Illness That Hits the Poor." *The New York Daily News*, May 12, 1989.

Robinson, Keith. "Twenty-Three-Year-Old Refugee $6 Million Lottery Winner." *Kennebec Journal*, November 18, 1989.

Rohrig, Byron L. "Lottery Foes Target Public Policy." *The Christian Century*, April 29, 1987.

Smothers, Ronald. "Tennessee Republicans See an Election Weapon in State's Bingo Scandal." *The New York Times*, January 28, 1990.

Thomas, William V. *Gambling's New Respectability*.

Weinstein, David, and Lillian Deitch. *The Impact of Legalized Gambling: The Socioeconomic Consequences of Lotteries and Offtrack Betting*.

Chapter 5

Ackermann, Todd. "Preying on the Poor." *National Catholic Register*, July 30, 1989.

Baker, Russell W. "Casinos Fail to Revive Atlantic City." *The Christian Science Monitor*, October 18, 1989.

Barron, James. "States Sell Chances for Gold As a Rush Turns to Stampede." *The New York Times*, May 28, 1989.

Becker, Gary S. "Higher 'Sin' Taxes: A Low Blow to the Poor." *Business Week*, June 5, 1989.

Colson, Charles. "The Myth of the Money Tree."

"Debate: Football Lottery Is an All-round Loser." *USA Today*, July 21, 1989.

Farmer, John J. "The Land of Odds." *The Star-Ledger*, September 17, 1989.

Harpaz, Beth J. "Revenue from Games Not Welcome By All." *Morris County Daily Record*, February 12, 1989.

Helm, Leslie. "Can Gtech Keep Winning at the Lottery?" *Business Week*, May 18, 1987.

"Inquiry. Topic: Hitting the Jackpot." *USA Today*, December 28, 1988.

Larini, Rudy. "Odds Go Against Having Megalottery in Jersey." *The Star-Ledger*, April 30, 1989.

"Lotteries: Even Winners Are Lucky to Break Even." *Money*, November 1988.

MacManus, Susan A. "State Lotteries Aren't a Windfall for Education." *The Wall Street Journal*, February 14, 1989.

Morison, Samuel Eliot. *The Oxford History of the American People*.

Painton, Priscilla. "Boardwalk of Broken Dreams." *Time*, September 25, 1989.

Porter, Sylvia. "Lottery Fever—Illness That Hits the Poor."

Rabushka, Alvin, and Mikhail S. Bernstam. "To Keep the Tax Promise, Try a Lottery."

Rosenthal, Andrew. "President Opens Legislative Drive." *The New York Times*, January 9, 1990.

Shapiro, Joseph P. "The Dark Side of America's Lotto-Mania." *U.S. News & World Report*, September 19, 1989.

Thomas, William V. *Gambling's New Respectability*.

"$2,885,181,319,134.72—and Counting." *The New York Times*, November 24, 1989.

Weinstein, David, and Lillian Deitch. *The Impact of Legalized Gambling: The Socioeconomic Consequences of Lotteries and Offtrack Betting*.

Will, George F. "In the Grip of Gambling." *Newsweek*, May 8, 1989.

Chapter 6

"Battle in Indiana Looms on Gambling." *The New York Times*, November 7, 1989.

Berman, Zachary M. "New York State's Lottery Has Reached the Point of Lunacy."

Colson, Charles. "The Myth of the Money Tree."

"Debate: Football Lottery Is an All-Round Loser." *USA Today*, July 21, 1989.

Egan, Timothy. "Oregon Inaugurates Football Betting." *The New York Times*, September 7, 1989.

Farmer, John J. "Ace In the Hole." *The Star-Ledger*, September 18, 1989.

Ford, Jesse Hill. "No Need for Lottery Lid; the More, the Merrier." *USA Today*, May 1, 1989.

"Inquiry. Topic: Hitting the Jackpot." *USA Today*, December 28, 1988.

Johnson, Dirk. "Gambling Returns to Town of Legend."

"Kentucky Drops Plans for Football Lottery." *The New York Times*, October 25, 1989.

Larini, Rudy. "Odds Go Against Having Megalottery in Jersey."

Magnusson, Paul. "A National Lottery Is Not Such a Long Shot."

Modern Maturity. American Association of Retired People, February-March 1990.

"NBA Attempts to Stop Lottery." *Kennebec Journal*, November 18-19, 1989.

"Not-So-Fine Print." *The New York Times*, November 27, 1989.

"Patriots Oppose Gambling Plan." *Kennebec Journal*, July 28, 1989.

Rabushka, Alvin, and Mikhail S. Bernstam. "To Keep the Tax Promise, Try a Lottery."

Rooney, Andy. "States Need a Better Way to Raise Funds." *Daily Record*, September 17, 1989.

Rose, I. Nelson. "Gambling's Fall: You Can Bet on It". *Los Angeles Times*, August 17, 1989.

Will, George F. "In the Grip of Gambling."

Further Reading

Adler, Bill. *The Lottery Book.* New York: Bill Adler Books, Inc., William Morrow and Company, 1986.

Findlay, John M. *People of Chance: Gambling in American Society from Jamestown to Las Vegas.* New York: Oxford University Press, 1986.

Jackson, Shirley. *The Lottery and Other Stories.* New York: Farrar, Straus, Giroux, 1949, 1982.

Peterson, Virgil W. *Gambling, Should It Be Legalized?* Springfield, Ill.: Charles C. Thomas 1951.

Weinstein, David and Lillian Deitch. *The Impact of Legalized Gambling: The Socioeconomic Consequences of Lotteries and Offtrack Betting.* New York: Praeger Publishers, 1974.

Index